From the Shade

The Letters of
Sister Gabriel Roeder, SSND

Edited by
Roberta E. Sabin

Design, Layout, & Printing by Uptown Press Inc.,

Baltimore, Maryland, USA

www.uptownpress.com

ISBN: 978-1-935911-59-3

Contents

About the Title

The title of this collection of letters derives from the phrase "Mure U Tiv," a title given by the people of Makar, Nigeria, in early 2002 to Sister Gabriel Roeder, SSND, as she prepared to move from the area after eight years' service there. In the Tiv language, "mure" means shade, much valued in sunny Nigeria. In the words of well-wishers at a farewell party for Sister Gabriel:

The Tiv people believe that Mure is their only solace after being beaten by the merciless African sun in their farms... You have brought hope to the helpless just like the shade brings comfort to the Tiv farmer from the merciless African sun.

Read on to learn more about the generous and tireless work of the woman who was called "Shade of the Tiv."

Preface

I was fortunate to live for several years with Sister Gabriel Roeder, SSND. Gabe, as she was known in her religious community, the School Sisters of Notre Dame, or Florence, as she was known to her family, was a remarkable woman: intelligent, energetic, open to new ideas, caring, and deeply and powerfully faith-filled. I was 22 when I met Gabe and found in her a model of the type of woman I hoped to become. After our paths separated in the early 70s, we continued occasional contact, and I followed from afar her adventures in Africa. After she returned to Baltimore in 2007, we met regularly, frequently sharing brunch at a favorite diner. I knew that hers was a story that should be shared.

This volume contains her letters sent stateside to family and friends during the second half of her assignment to Africa. Gabe's service in Nigeria began in 1977 and continued with two short interruptions until 2007, when health issues brought her home to Villa Assumpta in Baltimore. The letters here were written between 1990 and 2004. Most of the letters were handwritten. Some were typed and a few were emails. I apologize for any errors, especially in names of persons and places. Gabe and I had planned that she proofread all the files, but God had other ideas. Her death in August, 2019, cut short editing and, more importantly, the introductory material and commentary that she intended to write. She was able to complete the Introduction that follows.

May you enjoy sharing Gabe's adventuresome and giving spirit. Welcome to her world!

– Roberta Sabin
April 2021

▲ Florence Roeder and her family as she enters the
SSND community, September, 1956

Life Journey

1937: March 1, Florence Elizabeth Roeder born in Baltimore, fourth of seven children to George and Florence Hobbs Roeder, residents of Catonsville, Maryland

1955: graduated high school, the Institute of Notre Dame; president of her class

1955-56: attended the College of Notre Dame of Maryland (now the University of Notre Dame Maryland)

1956: entered the School Sisters of Notre Dame, where in 1957, she received the name Sister Mary Gabriel

1959: received a BA in mathematics and chemistry

1959-60: taught seventh grade at St. Joseph's School, Verona, Pennsylvania

1960-70: taught mathematics, chemistry, and religion at St. Maria Goretti High School, Hagerstown, Maryland

1970-76: served as Director of Vocations and Novices in Baltimore and at the Interprovincial Novitiate

1972: received an MA in theology from St. John's University, Collegeville, Minnesota

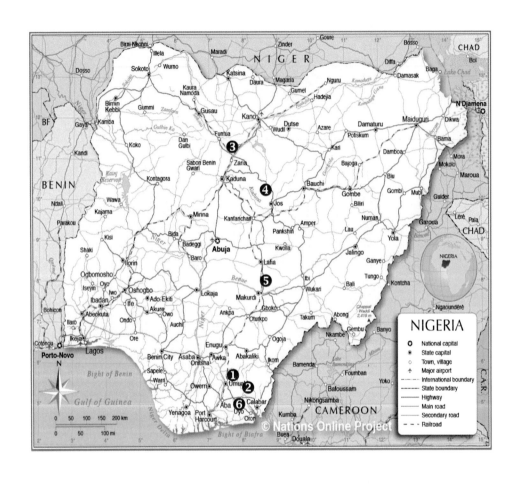

1976-77: studied at the Catholic Theological Union, Chicago, Illinois

1977-78: taught seminarians and secondary school students in Ikot Ekpene, south Nigeria ❶

1978-79: in Baltimore to care for her mother during her last illness

1979-80: studied Hebrew and taught at Notre Dame Preparatory School

1981-88: pastoral assistant at Pastoral Institute in Uyo and taught theology and scripture at Cross River State University in Calabar, south Nigeria; lived in the village Ikot Etuk Udo ❷

1989: sabbatical in Baltimore

1990-92: taught theology and scripture at Juniorate of St. Joseph Minor Seminary, Zaria, north central Nigeria ❸

1992-94: taught theology and scripture at St. Augustine Seminary, Jos, central Nigeria ❹

1994-2001: established Notre Dame Secondary School for Girls, Mkar, south central Nigeria ❺

2002-07: taught SSND postulants, Uyo, South Nigeria (near Calabar) ❻

2007-2019: in volunteer ministry and retirement, Villa Assumpta, Baltimore, Maryland.

◀ At the Institute of Notre Dame, 1955

Gabe at St. Maria Goretti, ▶ 1962, where she taught math, chemistry, and religion.

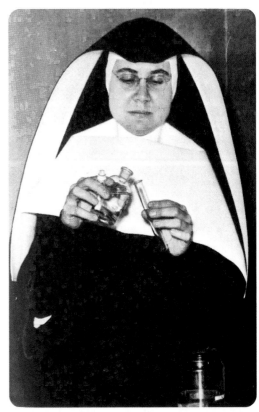

▲ Gabe with Sr. Melmarie Gentry, 1977

▲ Gabe (top row, third from left), as part of the first assembly
of SSND African missionaries in Nsawam, Ghana in 1981

Welcome to My World

1977-1990

Welcome to my world! – a stroll down memory lane in Nigeria with me! Through the process of writing "general letters" to family and friends while missioned in Nigeria, I was able to stay in touch with many family members and friends and unwittingly created material for a great journal. Folks were "charmed" by the unfamiliar content and kept the letters to share with others.

Why was I in Nigeria? Good question.

I am a School Sister of Notre Dame from Baltimore. For many of us, I believe, going to a "foreign mission" is always a great attraction. While I was participating in an international program in Rome in 1971, I met many Sisters of other congregations from around the world. Most were from Africa, especially East Africa. They would tell us how much they needed teachers there and invited us to come and help them so that they could help themselves. How tempting is that? They especially wanted teachers of math and science – and at the time, that was me! I wrote to my Provincial and ran the idea past her – and she said 'no.' I would be working in Formation.

A few years later, when we had a new Provincial, I tried asking again, but again the answer was still no. I was needed at home. Four years later, we again had a new Provincial. By this time, we had one Sister from our Province working in Nigeria, West Africa, – someone I knew and had lived with before. As God would have it, the Bishop of the Diocese where that sister worked stopped by the Motherhouse to visit the Provincial, so I chose this opportunity to meet and greet the Bishop and mention to my Provincial how I, too, was hoping to, someday, go to Africa. She said "Gabe, that's great!" Great, indeed! In Nigeria, they would say "God's time is the best time." So, after seven years of hoping and waiting, I began to prepare to go to Nigeria.

After a year's preparation of study in Mission Theology at Catholic Theological Union in Chicago in a marvelous program that included students from around the world, I went to Nigeria in 1977. I returned to the States finally in 2007, but if my body were in better shape, I would still be there. God knows my heart is still there. However, I thank God for everything that enabled me to go there to live among these wonderful people and to minister to them. They ministered to me as well – I learned so much from the people and their culture that I count myself greatly blessed. I wish everyone could have the opportunity of living for a while in another culture. You will recognize and appreciate your own culture in a new and wonderful way as well.

In 1977, I joined Sister Melmarie Gentry in the small village of Eriam where we taught part time in a Catholic Girls Secondary School on the same compound where we lived, and part time in a Catholic Boys Secondary School just a couple of miles down a very bad road. Both of these schools were considered minor seminaries. The Government had taken over the Catholic schools, so the Bishops had insisted they had to have some schools to prepare young people to consider becoming priests and sisters. Each Diocese was allowed to have one (Catholic) Secondary School for boys and one for girls, though only few graduates pursued a religious vocation. The Biafran war was still fresh in many minds, and the poverty and disease that were side effects of the war were still visible.

In June of 1978, S. Melmarie returned home and another Sister, previously missioned in Kenya, joined me. Shortly after, my mother had surgery for a brain tumor. I returned home for a visit during the summer and then went home again in November. My mother had gone into a coma when she received her chemotherapy. The day I arrived back, she came out of the coma, but she was paralyzed on one side. After some weeks, I decided I needed to stay to help care for my mother; the Sister back in Nigeria decided not to stay alone and returned to Kenya.

My mother died in May of 1979 and I was soon looking toward the possibility of returning to Nigeria. The Provincial Team at that time said I needed to wait until we could find some others to join me for the sake of stability in the community there. In January of 1981, a new group of three was ready to try again!

This time we lived in a different part of the Ikot Ekpene Diocese, but still in a small village – Ikot Etuk Udoh. The village was on a main road, midway between the two towns of Uyo and Ikot Ekpene; we were about 10 miles from each. The other two Sisters taught in a government Secondary School within walking distance of our house (if it was not too hot), while I was assigned to work in the Pastoral Center in Uyo. Uyo is in a different Diocese than Ikot Ekpene, so there was a Bishop in each place. The Pastoral Center was to serve the towns of Ikot Ekpene, Uyo and the town of Abak, which was part of Ikot Ekpene Diocese. The three towns formed a triangle joined by *very* bad roads. To make my life more exciting, I found the Pastoral Center without any furniture, supplies or resources. There was a young priest who was to work with me, but, like myself, he was not able to turn nothing into something either. I worked hard to prepare an Advent Program for the catechists in each town and began meeting with each group once a week when Advent started. Midway through, I was walloped with my first case of malaria. I woke up in the hospital with my sheets drenched from my sweat. Man proposes, God disposes!

Since there was no salary or stipend for my work, I took on a second job of assisting the teachers in a very large Catholic Primary School in Uyo, just next to the Pastoral Center. I was able to get children's bibles for each classroom and I was assisting the teachers with making bulletin boards. I was also working toward improving the environment of the school Masses that were held in the open hallway of the school; there was much to be desired to improve the situation. However, this idea got nipped in the bud when the Bishop of Ikot Ekpene heard that I was working for the Bishop of Uyo. Not O.K. I was told that if I needed a salary, I could try to get a job at the College of Education, which was in Uyo. This I did, and for the next seven years, I taught at this institution. The Education classes were huge, but I only taught in this program for a year or two. During that time, it became the University of Cross River State (Unicross) and I then taught scripture in the Religion Department. I must say that in spite of all the challenges and frustrations, I enjoyed teaching there. My scripture classes were small and I was able to get to know the students. Then, in 1989, I was given a year at home to rest and recoup.

"All the works of God proceed slowly and in pain, but then the roots are the sturdier and the flowering the lovelier."
– Mother Theresa

1990 brings us to the first of our "general letters!" While I was still Stateside, the Provincial Team asked me if I would be willing to move to the North (northern part of Nigeria) to look for a suitable place for an SSND mission. I was not surprised by the idea because the Apostolic Delegate to Nigeria had told us when members of the Provincial Team were visiting that the real needs of the Church in Nigeria were in the North – predominantly Muslim, but with many Catholic parishes nestled across the area. I was not very familiar with the North, nor did I know what the needs of the Catholics were. Father Sambo, a priest who was studying at the Seminary in Baltimore and whom I had met, suggested the minor seminary in Zaria as a good place to go. After the Team checked that out, it seemed the only good option. I agreed to go. It meant I would be living by myself – no other SSNDs for miles around. But by God's grace, I was assured a teaching position and a suitable place to stay by the Rector of the minor seminary in Zaria in Kaduna State.

Gabe
April, 2017

In January, 1981, the Baltimore SSND Province formally undertook ministry to Nigeria. Gabe and Sisters Virginia Brien and Dorothy Hunt, answered the call.

On January 13, we began our journey to Nigeria—arriving in our new village home on the 15th. On arriving in Port Harcourt. We were told that our house "was not ready." However, the Daughters of Charity welcomed us to stay [with them] in Uyo. We were there for about six months and joined the sisters there in all their activities.

Finally, we were able to move into our newly built home in the village of Ikot Etuk Udo. The home had a lovely chapel, three bedrooms, a dining/living room, a large kitchen, storage room and pantry as well as a bathroom equipped with toilet, washroom, and shower. We also had a garage, two latrines and a laundry room. In the beginning, we had no running water or electricity. We collected rainwater for all uses and burned candles or used kerosene lamps. Even with these inconveniences, we were happy.

We learned so much while we lived in Ikot Etuk Udo. We learned to relax, to let go and let God. We learned new ways of protecting and strengthening relationships, of extending hospitality, of sharing. And we learned that "God's time is the best time!"

– Sr. Virginia Brien, SSND
July, 2021

◄ Sister Gabriel with
Sisters Pat Flynn,
May Elizabeth
Semmelmeyer,
Dorthoty Hunt,
& Virginia Brien in
Ikot Ekpene, 1984

Circa 1994 ►
The "three"
from Baltimore:
Sisters Gabriel,
Virginia Brien,
& Dorothy Hunt

1990-1992

Teaching for a Growing Church

When Gabe returned to Nigeria in 1990, it was to an area of the country very different from where she had previously served. Her first assignments (1977-1989) were in the southeast section of the country, first in the Ikot Ekpene diocese, northwest of Uyo. In the southern state of Akwa Ibom, Ikot Ekpene is the political and cultural capital of the Annang ethnic group. There Gabe taught at the University of Cross River State in Calabar, in the diocese of Uyo. Both locations are in the same general region near the Cameroon border, have a sizable Christian population, and have a tropical monsoon climate.

After her return to Nigeria in 1990, she began teaching at a junior seminary in Zaria, in north–central Nigeria, northeast of Kaduna. This predominantly Muslim area has a very different climate from the southeast and a different ethnic heritage. This first segment of her letters begins with her arrival.

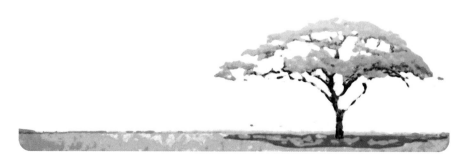

Letter One

Dear Family and Friends,

My greetings to everyone!

I've just had a lovely siesta and I'm now enjoying some tea and biscuits in my room here at the seminary in Zaria. Everyone has been very kind and welcoming, as Nigerians usually are.

My room is large, twice the size of the one I left. It opens onto a veranda, like a motel room, on the ground floor. Mine is the only one with a private shower and toilet. I also have a wide bed, a double I guess, with wooden supports for the mosquito net that make it look like a poster bed. There is a small fridge, a cupboard, table and chair and lounge chair and a walk in closet with shelves on one side. There is screening on the window and a ceiling fan. One Form V seminarian is appointed to take care of my needs and clean my room. Nice?! Fit for a queen!

On the other side of the coin, the place is poor and water is scarce. It looks bare and less spiffy than a convent – definitely a man's world. I will transform my own room in time! Needless to say, it is a joy to be here!

My trip was long. U.S Air left Baltimore one hour late because of a storm; KLM left N.Y. 2 hrs. late because of fog. We arrived in Amsterdam 10 min. before the connecting plane was to leave. We <u>ran</u> 1/2 mile to the gate and made the plane – which was waiting for us. When I arrived in Kono, I found my luggage did <u>not</u> make it. Next KLM flight is Monday!

On the last leg of the journey I met the superior general of Our Lady of Fatima congregation. One of their affiliates was at the airport to meet her who worked for Immigration. Do you know what I'm going to say next? I didn't even stand in line. He waited a few minutes and all was taken care of!

Two priests met me and helped me report my missing luggage. We dropped one priest there in Kono before driving on to Zaria. He will check on my luggage and phone us when it comes in. The drive here was about 1 1/2 to 2 hrs. When we arrived there was no NEPA – no electricity flowing. We weren't here 5 minutes when it came on! Although it was dark, there were several priests and others to greet me. We ate and walked around the compound. Fr. Emmanuel told me that during the riots in 1989, all but one building was burned. The priest who was rector at the time was away, but the boys and those here made no violent response to the action, although they lost their books and clothes. That restraint later made the Moslems to feel very ashamed of themselves. What a witness of <u>real</u> strength!

Fr. Emmanuel drove me around Zaria today. One woman brought me some tea, coffee, corn flakes, etc. The room was already equipped with dishes, tableware, electric kettle, etc.!

We are having evening Mass today and I hear the music and singing practice. I'll close here and go take some pictures. The flowering trees are in bloom and they are gorgeous. Be assured that I arrived safe and sound and I am in good hands! Thanks again to everyone for your wonderful kindness to me while I was home! I am well supplied with happy memories.

On Monday I hope to travel to Kaduna to see Archbishop Jatau and go to Immigration to "check in." I hope to be in touch again soon.

With lots of love,
Gabriel

Letter Two

Dear Family and Friends,

Greetings to each of you from Zaria!

I pray you are all well and enjoying life wherever you are!

My life here is beginning to settle into a bit of a routine. I've begun teaching math and Bible Knowledge. We have Mass at 6:30 a.m. on Tuesdays and Thursdays; 6:30 p.m. on Mondays, Wednesday, and Fridays; 6 p.m. on Saturdays and 7:45 a.m. on Sundays. There is a Mass in Hausa Sundays at about 10 – this is also the parish of St. Enda's since the burning of the churches in '87. At 6 p.m. on Sundays, the boys sing Vespers.

We haven't had much rain yet, but we have plenty of dust. Before the rain, the wind carries the dust everywhere. However, I now have <u>3</u> boys to help me sweep and dust my room everyday – Emmanuel, Absolom, and Joel. We tackle some of the other cleaning a little at a time. Except for Sundays, the 3 report everyday at about 7 a.m.

I eat breakfast in my own room and dinner and supper in the dining room. Dinner is around 2 p.m. and supper 8 or 9 p.m. – often by myself. The cook, Mousa, is doing his best to please me. When I passed up chicken the first day because it was too tough for my teeth, Fr. Emmanuel told Mousa to buy liver. I had liver at <u>least</u> once a day for the next week in a palm oil stew. In self defense, I went to the market and bought some tins of fish! the priests don't seem to eat vegetables very much, except beans. Once in a while carrots or string beans appear. I have to work on changes little by little. Right now I'm sill trying to get Mousa to bring me drinking water every day.

Zaria is much bigger than I thought it was. It is somehow more spread out than most cities. Its commercial section is not all that big, though it too is spread out. There are many (a dozen?) institutions of learning which bring people from all over, both as teachers and as students. There is a marvelous mixture of people here, many well educated. And then there are the beggars – hundreds and hundreds of them. They are outside the stores and supermarkets, at the filling stations. I'm told these are the people who were used to set fire to the churches. One woman told me that she won't give to the beggars anymore because of that. Fr. Emmanuel said one priest offers them matches! Fr. Emmanuel won't give them anything either but for a different reason. He says they all have families who could care for them and some could even work, but the prefer to beg. He says this is unfair to the Nigerians who are working during these economically tough times. So I haven't given even a kobo myself, but I find it hard. Some of the beggars are children, cripples, lepers, old folk...

Fr. Emmanuel is rector and pastor. He has one assistant, Fr. Francis, plus a deacon, Rev. Marinus, and 4 seminarians. Then, of course, there is a staff of lay people. At least 2 are Youth Corpers doing their year of service, one of whom is from Unicross in Uyo!

My driving license is renewed and I've driven around Zaria a bit, to Kaduna and back, and I went yesterday with Fr. Emmanuel to assist a catechist from Malumfashi who had been in an accident in the pick-up he was driving. The last leg of the good will journey was a gorgeous drive to Malumfashi – where I found my name in the guest book from 1981! The expanse of farmlands was impressive. As dusk came, the scene was so peaceful and idyllic, with cows grazing or a herd of sheep. The mud houses are quite different from those in the south; the dress is also different.

I've been getting to know people little by little. Our Sunday night ritual is to have supper with a Lebanese couple, Harry and Liz, who have extended an open invitation to the priests and sisters every week for 20 yrs! I'm the only sister in Zaria, but Liz is there and sometimes her lady friends or relatives are there, so there is some feminine presence. A couple of Irish priests come, the rest Nigerian priests.

One of the women in the parish, Mrs. Bowyer, married to an Englishman, checks on me regularly. Another woman, Bridget, also comes by. She and her friend Grace took me to market last Saturday – that's when I knew Zaria was <u>big</u>! And I've joined the CWO – Catholic Women's Organization, in St. Enda's parish. In Malumfashi I found out that there is a Sisters Area Conference for this region, though the next meeting is not until October.

The priests here have been wonderful. They all work so hard for their people. I can understand now why Fr. Sambo needed a rest. But they laugh and tease each other all the time!

Take care! I hope I can write again soon. My first letter came from Mary Ellen Holmes, sent on the 16th of May, arrived the 28th!

With lots of love,
Gabriel

Letter Three

June 25, 1990

Dear Family and Friends,

Sannu! My greetings to everyone! I pray all are well and finding a lazy pace of life during theses summer months.

I am well and settling in to the life here at the seminary in Zaria. We are in the midst of the 2nd term, which ends on July 30th. We have a 3 week break before returning for the final term.

The rains are increasing and the earth is responding with a glow of green from corn stalks, rice fields, etc. The rains were late coming and I've heard that Kano has had none yet. Thus far, the rains have always come with storms, so the electricity is turned off. Typical of town life, folks are not well prepared for alternatives, so everything stops. I have a candle, though sometimes a student may bring one of the gas lamps from chapel.

The seminary is situated on the Old Kano Road. The stretch of it alongside our property is checkered with pot holes. When the dilapidated trucks pass by, it sounds for all the world like they are falling apart. Many lorries (trucks) use the road at night. The rumbling of the trucks, the barking of the 2 watchdogs, the roosters and owls created a strange symphony to my ears and woke me often during the night. I'm now sleeping through most of that and the rising bell besides! My own alarm clock is back on duty.

The deacon, Marinus, and I were able to get to Abuja over this past weekend for the ordination of 14 young men for the Missionary Society of St. Paul. This year, for the first time, they will be sending some of their priests to Botswana, in south Africa. It was a beautiful ceremony and an exciting day in the life of the Nigerian Church. After only 6 years, the society has ordained 54 men. This society is comparable to our Maryknoll. People came from far and wide in Nigeria, by bus taxi and private cars. Some people had travelled 11 hours. Parishes from Tagos to Calabar came out to support their newly ordained and celebrate with him.

It was also a chance for me to see some familiar faces. I received a warm welcome from H.E. Cardinal Ekandem, John McGuiness SPS – 50 years ordained, Brian Byrne SPS and lots of others. They were surprised to see me and find that I am, now in Zaria. My own journey to Abuja was 4 hours each way, plus some added time in lay-overs. Because of that, we didn't stay in Abuja as long as we would have liked, but I promised to go back. The last leg of the journey home was by taxi at night – an initiation by fire!

A good segment of the journey was through heavy rain – at 70 or 80 mph! I prayed!

Father Emmanuel introduced me to a young Hungarian woman who lives in a nearby parish. She has been here with her husband and is going on a home visit next month for the first time in 12 years. Father told me later that she has access to a swimming pool, to which we are invited any time! He has never gone because he doesn't know how to swim, but he promised to take me sometime.

The struggle for water is still the toughest part of life here. On days when there is no water at any tap on the compound, the boys walk to the town to fetch water sometimes for the staff, sometimes for the kitchen, sometimes for themselves. It's part of the rhythm of life. And if ever you wanted extra water, this is the place – extra dust and sweat, zillions of flies from the many cattle here (horses too, and donkeys!), the presence of disease so typical of the tropics.

I'm very grateful to everyone who helped me with the mail chain. Letters are beginning to come in response to them. Today I received one from Maris mailed just one week ago – in St. Cloud, Minnesota! It's always good to hear news from home. Little by little, I'm writing individual letters, but the general letter helps a lot.

Many of my math students are very poor. With some it is laziness, but with others, it is because of a poor foundation in some little bush school. This afternoon I gave a test for those who were absent for the 1st assessment test 2 weeks ago. Three fellows who had taken the test and failed asked to retake it. When I said I could correct it for them, but not count it, they were quite happy. I've been having some classes in the afternoon to drill the basics, and almost all of them (70+) come – usually from games or afternoon labor! Do pray for them – and me!

Take care! My greetings to all!

With love and prayers,
Gabe

Letter Four

July 16, 1990

Dear Family and Friends,

Sannu! Time flies when you're having fun! – and I hope each of you is having fun where ever you are!

The rector gave the students the week off as a mid-term break from July 2nd to 5th. He had ulterior motives, one of which was for the students to get the remainder of their school fees. He "can't run the school on Hail Marys!" The second reason was that the latrine needed to be cleaned (emptied?) and the sanitation department's machinery was broken – so it had to be done by laborers. It took four young men a day and a half to dig a pit to bury the refuse. By the end of the week, that project was completed. The students who returned the following Monday, however, did not have their fees complete, so – a good number were sent right back home. Some are still being sent back this week.

During this next-term break, I had a chance to go to Kano to visit the St. Louis sisters there while the rector went to a meeting, (The indigenous priests meet together every month; this month it was to discuss AIDS). The secondary school for girls, run by the St. Louis sisters, is by far the nicest I've seen in Nigeria. It was taken over by the government after the Civil War and now has a mosque on the compound for the large Moslem population of students (80%). It is administered by the sisters and the cooperation between Christian and Moslem is reflected in the peaceful and pleasant atmosphere.

There were over 1200 applications for the entrance exam for next year, and they only take about 100. The school is a real tribute to the educational vision of the sisters!

I met 2 Irish sisters, Maura and Bridgette, and 3 young Nigerian women in formation. There was time to swap ideas, see their convent, enjoy dinner with the sisters and have a siesta before the rector's meeting finished. I also met a few new faces among the priests who had gathered.

The Kano trip was on the 4th of July. On the 5th, the rector and I set out for southern Kaduna. This area had been suggested by Father Sambo as one we might be interested in for a convent. We drove south from Zaria, past the city of Kaduna, into the most gorgeous, green farmland! For hours, we sailed along good roads with a view of lush fields, so far as the eye could see. Some farms had big herds of cattle – a new sight for me here, since I always see the cattle in small bunches being driven to market.

We stopped in Zonkwa, where the St. Louis sisters have another convent. Because there are so very few convents in this area, these sisters do <u>overtime</u> in the ministry of hospitality for travelers, and it is warmly and graciously rendered! As we travelled south, we had also travelled <u>up</u> as we approached the Kamoro Hills and Plateau State, so I slept under a blanket in Zonkwa! Each day, Father Emmanuel and I set out, after Mass with the sisters, to touch some of the parishes in the towns – Kachia, Kafunchan, Kamoro, etc. The area is predominantly Christian, strongly Catholic, though there are some Moslems there. Between the towns were wonderful stretches of farmland. The towns which had local government headquarters were the ones Father pointed out as likely spots for a school. We met many, many people along the way, including Father's family. His father had 4 or 5 wives, so the family is large. When his father asked for baptism, he chose 1 wife to marry in the Church and entrusted the others to their eldest sons. He had to move out of the compound where the other wives lived, so he built another house across the road. All the wives and their children became Catholic as well. Father has a cousin and a nephew, also priests.

There are about 7 different tribes in the area, each with their own language, but all speaking Hausa as well. The people were very friendly, as they are in Ikot Etuk Udo. On Sunday, Father celebrated Mass in a parish in Kachia for one Irish father who was down with typhoid. The church was small and so poor—as were the people, but the benches were packed with singing, happy folks! He had a wedding of a young couple during the Mass—no special clothes or festivities. The young woman was several months pregnant, and both were shy and happy as the focus of attention. After Mass, the people asked Father to introduce himself and me, which he did, in Hausa. Later, outside, two men came to ask what kind of school we might have, because they were very interested in being partners with us!

We returned to Zaria loaded down with young palm trees, grapefruit, guava and sweet memories of the pleasant episodes of our journey!

By now, I'm up to my ears in school work, preparing for exams next week and my next trip—to Port Harcourt, for the African Assembly, by the week's end.

Thanks so much to all who have written in response to this general letter!—You are noble, indeed! It has been great to hear news of you, and little by little, I'll answer individually, too. In spite of the typhoid around, I am very well, thank God. (I was vaccinated against typhoid!) I caught a cold from the chilly air that follows the rains here—would you believe I'm wearing a sweater right now?! I'm told there was finally rain in Kano, so people there are happy—relieved for the relief from the heat and water for the farms.

We have school break after exams for 3 weeks. School resumes around August 27th. I'll be in Port Harcourt. and Uyo for the first part of the break; then in Kaduna to see Archbishop Jatau and see what possibilities are there for us. My plan is to be home by August 17th – I promised to give a vocation talk on the 18th. Father Emmanuel asked me to help spruce up the small chapel upstairs, so I may try to make some curtains before school opens. And, of course, God willing, I may write another letter!

God's blessings on all, especially those with birthdays or anniversaries!

With lots of love,
Gabe

Letter Five

19 August 1990

Dear Lois, Carolyn and Joe,

Hi! Greetings to each of you from Zaria!

I hope you are all well and finding time for some R + R during the hot days! This past Tuesday I returned from our African Assembly in Port Harcourt and a few days in Uyo. The days here are lazy because school is not in session, but there is plenty to do. The rector is trying to spiff up the small chapel here in the Father's House, and I'm trying to help, mostly with sewing. We still have one more week before the boys come back.

Lois, thanks for your letter with news about Robert. Ruth had written a few weeks ago, and I sent a get well card and a note to him $^c/_o$ your address. Did it ever come? So much of my mail gets lost that it's frustrating!

Thanks so much for the article on Cathy Arata and the World Summit for Children. I've written a note to the Chief whose name and address you enclosed to see what he is doing. (I don't know him – there are hundreds of chiefs in every state, and we have 21 states!). I'll talk to the rector about possibilities here.

Thanks so much for relaying the general letters I'm sending out. I hope to get another one ready this coming week. I do appreciate the time, energy and postage, paper, etc.! The names missing from your list are Angie Flynn, Ginny Neimeyer, Alice and Walter, Uncle Ormy, Aunt Virginia et. al. (if they are interested), Padraig Flanigan, and you could add Howard Eichmiller, 372 Greenmount Ave, Balto. 21218. I don't have Patty Woods address until she writes – she was to leave the camp address in early August.

Father Brian Byrn gave me a book to read on the Enneagram by Don Richard Riso, and, Lois, I think you are a seven in his book! Maybe you could get a copy of his book at the library if you're interested. If you can't I could xerox the pages and mail them.

The African Assembly was just great! We had 2 of our Polish sisters who are now working in the Gambia there. One of our Japanese sisters is a general councilor and she came along with Pat Flynn from Rome, so we had a more international flavor than usual. Having our own Nigerian postulants was, of course, special. The 2nd group of another 5 postulants has already been received! The postulancy in Uyo is very nice! And in a good location, too.

Carolyn and Joe, now that you can write letters on your word-processors, I hope I'll be receiving some from you! How is P.C. Partners doing? The rector has the attachment for videos for his T.V., though he doesn't seem to get many good movies. He has a lot of religious ones, some rough ones. I've seen "Exodus" and "Passage to India" (2nd time) plus 1 or 2 of the religious ones that are just fair. The machine can play videos from any country. I'll have to get David to make a video for me at one of the family gatherings! If you ever see any good ones on sale, I'd love to have one.

It certainly was great that Robert and Libby could stay with you while Robert was going through his surgery. I'm sure they were happy for the comfort of hospitality with family rather than a hotel in a strange city. One of the blessings inside an otherwise hard experience!

I feel like I've forgotten something I wanted to say but my brain is a bit tired tonight. Please give my greetings to everyone! Take care, and THANKS for all the good things you do!

Lots of love,
Florence

Letter Six

September 2, 1990

Dear Family and Friends,

Sannu! Greetings to everyone! I pray you are all well and finding joy in the life and happiness around you!

Daily life here in Zaria continues to keep me busy and makes the time fly by, even though school has not resumed yet. We have one more week of leisure before the boys return.

Our 5th SSND African Assembly in Port Harcourt was a wonderful experience. It was just great to be with SSND friends, and we had an added international flavor with our 2 Polish sisters from the Gambia, Sr. Maureen (Japan), our General Councilor who came with Pat Flynn, and, of course, our 5 Nigerian postulants. The input and sharing were rich; the hospitality of CIWA and the facilitation of Sr. Bernadette Okura SHCJ were marvelous.

Sr Loreen, Liberia, gave us stories and perspectives on the war there and increased our sensitivity to our own political situation. As usual, we all came away hungry for more!

After the assembly I spent a few days in Uyo and saw the beautiful new Postulancy building. It was good to go back to my old stomping ground. I took a bus from Uyo to Kaduna – 12 hrs. with one 1/2 hour stop. I ate and drank as little as possible! After reaching Kaduna, I stayed there a few days to meet with Archbishop Jatau. I managed to see part of the museum on one of those days, which has made me curious to visit some of the places around here that are well-known for their arts or crafts. Nok is a town famous for its prehistoric sculpture, and is located in southern Zaria. Since this museum visit, I've managed to get myself invited to a 3 – day festival there in April, and I'm looking forward to it! I also found out that one of the women in the Catholic Woman's Organization is Yoruba and does sculpture, pencil sketching, tie-dye and batik.

Since my return to Zaria, I've spent most of my time sewing and cleaning. The rector wants the small Blessed Sacrament chapel here in the Father's House redone. It is quite lovely, with what he could afford. I'm still trying to find material for altar linens, but what I've managed to make so far are not really satisfactory. Linen is not to be found and the poly-cotton has too much poly. I can't find the flat white bias tape used for amices either. It seems the Irish fathers always bring linens back from their home visits, but they don't go very far. I'll keep on trying! On one of the shopping days, I had a great visit to Kano – a really nice city! I was told it was the southern end of the Sahara camel trade route, and so has always been a commercial center. It makes Zaria look dumpy, but then our main industry here is education; it is not really a commercial center.

We've also enjoyed a couple excursions with the Rector during these past weeks – one to A.B.U. Book shop, one to their Fine Arts Dept., and one to Mairuwa Dam at Funtua, a town about an hour's drive north of here. Because we are still getting rain, the countryside is green and gorgeous still.

In between other activities, I've tried to spruce up some of the potted flowers around the verandas of the house that are choking themselves or whose roots have broken their pots. It is good exercise but often people come to "relieve" me of the work when they see me doing it. Even when I'm hanging out my wash, it seems to embarrass people that I'm working!

While the painter was around for the chapel renovations, the top half of my bathroom wall was painted (the bottom has white tile). It is a sunshine-green oil paint which will make it easy to clean. I have a small wicker cupboard of 3 shelves (open) in the bathroom and it was painted the same sunshine green.

Mousa, the cook is doing really well providing me with a variety of menus, vegetables and tender meat! Theresa Bowyer faithfully sends fresh fruits and I shop for the makings of breakfast and supper. The day I was in Kano, I had a real ice cream cone!

I've been asked to meet with the Catholic girls at the Federal Girls Government College just next door to the seminary. I'm to go every Friday evening to give them any instruction, make sure they've received all the sacraments they should have, and help them prepare the Mass to be held on Saturday evening. They have just started the school, so they have only the first 2 forms – comparable to 7th + 8th grades. There are 200 or so girls in all, half Muslim and half Christian about 20 of whom are Catholic. My extra-curriculars keep increasing! Even the four Sisters who are students in Zaria get these kinds of responsibilities. The harvest is so great!

Everyone take care! Thanks so much for praying for mail. I promise to answer eventually!

Lots of love,
Gabriel

Letter Seven

Sept. 10, 1990

Dear Ange,

Hi! Dear Friend! Thanks so much for your last letter. I do hope you are getting copies of my general letters from Lois – if not, be sure to ask her or Carolyn now and again.

You've been on my mind – and in my heart— a lot these past weeks. I know Mike must be around by now. Your decision to ask him to let yourselves get re-acquainted again, with a counselor, sounds so very wise and so full of courage! I know God is leading you gently and surely. My guess is that Mike will be looking to you and leaning on you as a significant link with his own past life, so whatever you say will be of great influence. You will stay in my heart and in my prayers, Ange!

I am also concerned about <u>your</u> anxiety that you might be getting Alzheimer's. Do you have a regular physician who keeps tabs on you? I'm sure you've shared your concern with Marg and Mary and the kids. It is good to be free and open about it so that others will be alert. I don't want anything to happen to you, dear heart!

The boys came back yesterday, so <u>today</u> they began working on the Timetable!! No classes today. We had a staff meeting – someone reported from a workshop on how to make good tests. I'm still trying to finish up the little projects I've started, so after I did my own laundry, I did some "church" wash and worked on making a few more finger-towels, etc. from old altar-cloths. Tedious and time consuming!

I'm reading a book on African Art which I love. I'm surrounded by tribes which have produced <u>centuries</u> of artwork. To find it and appreciate it is the challenge.

I miss you, too, Ange. We did have lots of great times together. It was so good to share so many things with you! I miss our Group, too. Do give them all my love. I'll get around to writing soon – in the meantime, please share my general letters with them. My love to Mike and the kids. I hope they are all doing well. Take care, Angie! You are a beautiful and special person – to me and to lots of others!

With love and prayers,
Gabe

Letter Eight

October 28, 1990

Dear Family and Friends,

Sannu! My greetings to everyone! I pray you are all well and finding joy in all you do.

I feel a bit behind myself and unable to catch up – not an unfamiliar feeling for me. Too many irons in the fire!

Three weekends ago, I travelled to Akwa Ibom by bus to be present for the reception of our first Nigerian novices and visit with everyone there. I was really happy that I went and was able to share in the festivities. Needless to say, it was good to see everyone and taste the sweetness of community life among women!

Because of school, I stayed only 2 1/2 days, but they were good days, indeed.

The bus trip down was long and tiring. I left Zaria 5:30 p.m. on Thursday and reached Uyo around 4 p.m. on Friday. However, the return was worse. I found a bus that left Uyo 5:30 Monday morning, to reach Zaria by 6 a.m. the next morning. Since the trip down required a taxi and then a cycle for the last leg of the journey, one vehicle from beginning to end looked good. Looks are deceiving. The bus left Uyo shortly after 7 am and went first to Calabar – in the opposite direction of Zaria – where we waited for 1 hr. Then we headed north. After riding about 3 hrs we had a flat tire that took 1 1/2 hrs. to fix. We rode for about 2 hrs. and had another flat tire. It took only 1/2 hr. to fix it this time. We drove another hour and had the 3rd flat tire. We stayed there, slept in the bus, and in the morning the driver sent to <u>Calabar</u> for new tires. We milled around all day. I found a woman who helped me get some water to bathe myself, and passed the time reading *Reweaving Religious Life* which Marie de Chantal had sent me via Christine.

I don't usually take cooked food on the road because the eating utensils are normally washed in cold water and I'm afraid of germs. My fare was biscuits and soft drink, + bananas if there were any. A couple of people had expressed concern that I had not eaten and suggested I look for a Catholic Mission. Food was <u>not</u> my problem! My derriere was so sore, and I can't sleep on a bus, so I felt out of sorts generally. That evening the driver came to me and offered me a malt drink and a package of biscuits! He hardly spoke, but the Hausa people have the most beautiful and reverential way of giving or receiving anything. The item is held in 2 hands and the person does a curtsey or semi-genuflection. I was surprised and touched. I knew the man was a Muslim because I had seen him take his prayer mat onto the grass when we stopped for fuel on Monday evening. We were given time to buy something to eat, and the driver had gone aside, washed his hands, and knelt and bowed with head to the ground in worship. He is one of many persons here whose names I don't know, who I will never see again, but who have touched me in an indelible way.

Around 9 p.m., the new tire came. It was changed and we travelled to Makurdi, where we parked for the night. At 5 a.m., life stirs here, and so did I. The nice young man next to me helped me find a taxi that would carry the bamboo bench I was taking to Zaria and I left Makurdi about 7 a.m. By 11 a.m. I was in Kaduna and at 12:30 p.m. I was back home. Taxis drive about 140 km/hr, so my heart is always in my throat, but that seems to be the best way to travel – best meaning it wastes the least amount of time and money.

So with my tired body and happy memories, I jumped back into my routine here, but I've never caught up with myself!

Last weekend, the Sisters Area Conference for Sokoto/Kaduna Diocese met in Kaduna. Because people must travel far, it only meets twice a year. One sister drove 8 hrs by herself to come. We were 25 in all for a Friday evening and Saturday morning with Sr. Bernadette Okure SHCJ (who was with us at the African Assembly). The theme was Inculturation in Community and it was marvelous. The group is collegial – no president! It was a very informal, relaxed and friendly group and I did enjoy being with them! I'm beginning to miss community and miss the presence of women with the same interests – in case you can't tell!

After the meeting, I visited with some American Dominicans and we had lunch and shopped in the big city before 2 of them drove me to Zaria on their was back to Sokoto.

Today we had our parish Thanksgiving – Bazaar. Mass was 4 hrs. During the Offertory, every group possible was called to come and process to the altar with money or gifts – dancing and singing, of course! Married couples, Church Council, English Choir, Hausa choir, civil servants, teachers, prayer groups, various tribal groups, state groups – and their supporters. Some people got up almost every time, and loved it! After Mass, everyone went home to eat and came back around 3 for the Bazaar. The gifts brought in the morning – maize, soya beans, sugar cane, cocks, yams, were auctioned off. Each of the church groups was selling food to eat but you had to make a donation. Initially this was done over a microphone – an amount would be given to a group to "open" their plate. Some people made free donations. There was some cultural dancing too. They were trying to teach me. While my feet are not agile enough to keep up with them, they enjoy my joining them. It is 9:30 p.m. and I still hear a few voices outside. A good time seems to be had by all!!

I have to give "Continuous Assessment" tests this week, and I still have 35 math exercise books to go through. There is lots of work, but teaching is often fun in spite of the work. I still enjoy teaching math, after many years away from it. So, if you don't hear form me often, it's only because I can't balance all my acts together. School is over for the year at the end of November, so I can come up for air then!

Have a Happy Thanksgiving!

Lots of love,
Gabriel

Letter Nine

13 December 1990

Dear Family and Friends,

Sannu! A Merry Christmas and Happy New Year to all! I pray this letter will reach, at least some of you, during the Christmas

Season. However, if not, you know that I am thinking of you as I celebrate here.

Sister Sharon Dei was here for about a week and we had a most enjoyable and productive visit. The time flew by all too quickly, but everyday was a good one. Since Sharon left, I've been working with the Catholic Youth preparing for their National Convention which begins tomorrow. Today, they have a leadership workshop for the officers. Since I am chaplain for the Zaria Deanery and the Convention is being held here at the Seminary, I need to be available to help in whatever way I can. So, although know I will be interrupted, I've decided I had better start this letter or it will never get written!

My plan for Christmas is to go to Akwa Ibom and spend a couple of weeks with the Sisters. I will leave here after the Convention is over and when I get a few things done here for myself. If all goes well, that will be around the 18th of December. On the way back to Zaria, I plan to go to Jos to visit the OLF Sisters (Our Lady of Fatima) at their Novitiate. If time permits I may branch to Abuja. The new students for the seminary will be coming on Jan. 6th and the rest on Jan.13th, so I need to be back within that week.

The Rector has hired a young man solely to look after the Church and Chapel and do the church wash. If time allows, he is to keep the parlor clean. Since I had been overseeing that when the students were here, the new worker, James, was put under my supervision. He is a hard worker, but, like the seminarians, he thinks cleaning means sweeping, and he tends to do everything quick-quick. Since this boy could relieve me a big area of concern I've been trying to take time with him to teach him all I know about cleaning – but it takes much time. I am happy that the Rector sees the need to have one person responsible for the church work, and that the effort to keep things looking clean and nice in spite of the daily dust from the harmattan is worthwhile. I want to ensure that James can sail by himself while I'm away!

Well, the first interruption lasted most of the day! I've been in the pick-up truck more than I've been out of it – hauling mattresses, yams, corn for grinding, corn already ground, shopping. Since very few people showed up this morning for the leadership workshop, we are supposed to have something this evening. It is already 8:45 p.m. and nothing has begun!

The weather has been getting hotter; the afternoon sun scorches you like a hot iron if you are just standing in it. I can understand why people would prefer to keep their skin covered! The mango trees are beginning to flower and give off their sweet perfume of promise. There are MANY, MANY mango trees around this area. In spite of the heat and dryness, there is still green to be seen in the countryside. Some people are harvesting rice now while others are planting wheat, thanks to irrigation farming. The poinsettias are in bloom, a point in common with Christmas in the States. Here, though, they are not cultivated in pots, but grow in bushes. And dust is everywhere. I'm still waiting for the weather to turn cold! Sr. Sharon said the savannah here reminds her of the "green desert" in the States. The solitary hills of rock that pepper the landscape reminded her of Arizona.

Sister Sharon and I met so many people on our journeys that were hosts or hostesses to us, and so many kind and considerate taxi drivers or other persons who helped us along the way! I feel I owe many thank you notes to people to recognize their kindnesses and hospitality. We also enjoyed some "serendipitous" happenings which let us know once again that God works in wonderful ways. One of these took place on our journey from Port Harcourt to Zaria. Having arrived in Lagos from Port Harcourt in good time, we found the flight for Kaduna filled. The only other flight was at night, which I wanted to avoid, so we took a flight for Abuja with the intention of getting a taxi for the rest of the way. This plane was to leave at 1 p.m, so I expected to reach Zaria before dark. Well, the plane left about 3:30, so we only reached Abuja at 4:30. We could only get to Kaduna by 7:30 via taxi, which we did. All the way, I kept wondering if we would have been wiser to have just waited for the late Kaduna flight. My second-thoughts were somewhat dispelled by Sharon's delight in the contrast of scenery while we were in the taxi from Abuja to Kaduna, but the best was yet to come. In Kaduna we stayed at the Cath. Social Center. While at supper, we met people who were participants in a communications workshop being conducted at the Media Center (on the same grounds). This is Sharon's field, so the animated conversation led the participants to urge Sharon to go meet the Director, an American Jesuit, Fr. McFarland. This we did and we had a delightful visit. Father is 72 years old and spent most of his life in India, so he knows Fr. Kennedy, Fr. Guidera, etc. The sharing between him and Sharon led to Father inviting Sharon to help teach the summer 1991 workshop! It was a marvelous connection for Sharon, and we felt certain that taking the plane to Abuja had been part of God's and Theresa's doings! And if I see Sharon here next summer, that notion will be confirmed all the more!

It seems that after every journey there are stories to tell. I'm only sorry there isn't time and space for more. I need to close and work on the next step of getting photostat of this in the mail.

The convention is still in process. It is not National, but Archdiocesan. Kaduna Province covers about 2/3 of Nigeria space-wise!

Once more, my best wishes to everyone for the holiday season!

With love and prayers,
Gabriel

Letter Ten

16 January 1991

Dear Family and Friends,

Sannu! And best wishes for a happy and peaceful New Year! All is well here. In spite of the fact that the American Consulate in Kaduna is closed for fear that Muslims will retaliate against America here because of Kuwait, all is calm and normal. Someone said even the Embassy in Lagos is closed, but I don't think such panic is necessary. I'm in good hands here and quite safe.

It was wonderful over the Christmas holidays, and ever since, getting lots of mail – more than usual, anyway. Thanks so much to all who wrote! Hopefully this general letter will do until I'm able to respond individually.

You will enjoy hearing of my latest episodes on public transport. My journeys all seem full of adventure. On Dec 20th I finally got myself ready to travel to Akwa Ibom for the holiday. I left with Adamu, the driver, at 4:30 a.m. for the Motor Park (taxi-center) in Kaduna. We arrived shortly after 5:30 a.m. to find the place hopping with activity, even in the dark. You could hardly move around to find the taxi or bus you wanted – It was like a big market.

When I asked for Uyo in Akwa Ibom, I was directed to a bus that was leaving as soon as it was full, and only a few seats remained. The fare was double the usual fare because of Christmas, as I had been warned. I boarded the bus and we left a little after 7 a.m. Ah well!

When we reached Agbor, just outside of Onitsha, the bus broke down. As we milled around on the side of the road waiting to see what would happen, a Catholic woman, Rose Elemi, made herself known to me. After chatting, I told her there was a convent in Agbor (Daughters of Charity) and I was thinking of just going there for the night. It was already 4 p.m. and we had a good 5 hrs. to go. So Rose accompanied me as I went looking for a taxi or motorcycle that knew where the convent was. The taxi didn't go that way and the cyclist said it was a bit far. Rose discouraged me from going and invited me to accompany her, since she would be staying with her sister in Aba that night. I agreed, and with that, another bus came along, going only as far as Onitsha, but we grabbed our luggage and boarded it. We payed another fare, smaller, of course, and reached Onitsha as dark descended. Onitsha is like New York, – it never sleeps.

We quickly found a 3rd bus headed for Aba, boarded and paid another fare. We had gone less than an hour when that bus broke down. We were in front of a small place that sold cold drinks and bread. I got down and had something to eat and drink, but Rose was tired and stayed on the bus to sleep. The electricity went off, so there were only candles lighting our night plus the occasional lights from passing cars. After 30 or 40 minutes, another bus stopped and agreed to carry the passengers from the lame bus. There was a great hustle in the semi-darkness as much luggage got transferred, but Rose and I boarded bus #4, paid another fare, and were off for Aba.

We had gone only 15 minutes or so when Rose realized she had left her purse on bus #3. She shouted and called to the driver in the front of the bus to stop and go back but we kept sailing along. Rose was on her way to see her mother who was in the hospital and was seriously ill. The doctor suspected snake bite but had no serum. It was Rose who was able to find the serum so she was carrying this (on ice!) as well as money to help pay for the hospital bills. So she shouted and cried for the driver to stop, saying she had over $1,000.00 in her purse. The driver wouldn't stop. I tried to comfort the woman and pray with her, urging her to be calm and see what God would do.

When we came to a filling station, the bus pulled over. People encouraged Rose to get off and find a motorcycle to go back and look for her purse. Four or five people passed $10 notes so she could still reach Aba that night. We quickly arranged that I would keep her luggage and the serum and go to her sister's in Aba and wait. The people around helped me repeat the address over and over as I had no pen + paper handy. I had seen some of these people helping out strangers who had run out of money after bus #2 or 3, so I was very touched by the genuine concern and beautiful generosity. It was a real Christmas story, but in Nigeria, it can happen <u>any</u> day!

Well, Rose was all set to get off the bus when one woman warned her that the area was full of rogues. If she valued her life more than her $1,000.00, she should stay on the bus – and stay she did!

We reached Aba around 11 p.m., reported the lost purse and went straight to Rose's sister. We were warmly welcomed and well cared for. Early the next morning, Rose went to see her mother, who had greatly improved and gone to the bus terminal where her purse had been handed in with not a kobo missing! As I completed my journey to Uyo, my heart was full of praise and thanksgiving. Without the mishaps, we should never know how many good people surround us and how much good news goes unpublished!

My days in Akwa Ibom were full of Christmas get-togethers, old friends and good chats with everyone. The days flew by all too fast. I received word that my father was sick and called home. Daddy had pneumonia but had improved after being admitted to the hospital. Thanks to all who helped that message to find me! (No small thing, here!!)

On January 2, I got a bus for Jos to make my retreat there in an area called Kuru. Actually, I thought it was Bukuru. We got as far as Lafia, about 2 1/2 hrs outside of Jos and – would you believe? – the bus broke down. As we were milling around on the side of the road from 4 p.m. until after 5 p.m., I was asking people if anyone knew where Bukuru was, and could I reach it before dark. Two or three people offered to accompany me, but advised that it was better to spend the night at a convent in Jos. A car pulled up which we thought was a taxi looking for fares, so a group of us walked over to it. After greeting us, the man inside asked <u>me</u> if I was going to Jos. I said 'yes'. He said "I'll take you, Sister. I'm a reverend Father." I must have looked a little uncertain, because he pulled out his I.D. for me to see. So I was taken to Kuru, right to the door of the Novitiate of Our Lady of Fatima sisters! As it turned out, Kuru is about 30 miles <u>before</u> you reach Jos – what a blessing! And by the time we reached there, it was about 8 p.m., dark and COLD. God takes care of fools and nuns, as the saying goes!

Well, I'm settled back in Zaria, waiting for school to get started. We are going to try homogeneous grouping in the Junior High math. There are seventy some students, and they are being divided into 2 groups – those about 35 and those below 35 in their final grade! Before they were in 2 groups by homeroom. We'll see what happens!

At the staff meeting, I was given a couple more responsibilities. My teaching load will not be be similar to last year's, but there have to be some changes because of the homogeneous grouping and because the 2nd stream has now reached Form IV, which I teach Bible Knowledge to.

The harmattan is here – cool and pleasant temperatures in the day, chilly to cold at night, <u>dry</u> air, frequent breezes and DUST. Cleaning my room is a major event every day!

Sames, the new cleaner, is trying hard. Workers from the Diocesan Water Project are here, trying to dig 3 wells. A new storage building is going up to house the grain – which used to be kept in the extra classrooms. Lots of activity everywhere.

Take care! My greetings to all!

With love and prayers,
Florence (Gabriel)

Letter Eleven

15 March 1991

Dear Family and Friends,

Sannu! And Easter Joy to each one! I pray that the abundance of God's life and love may be fruitful in you!

Yesterday was a red-letter day. We heard thunder in the afternoon, and lo! We had our first brief shower in the evening. This evening we have rain again, for 2 hrs. so far. Praise the Lord! The last 2 days had been dreadfully hot, I think because it had gotten a bit humid. We have no light, but nobody seems to mind – the sound of the rain is very sweet. Yesterday's short shower helped lots – cooling the air and curtailing the dust. Tomorrow should be heaven!

In addition to the rain, I got a bundle of mail yesterday. Mail has been super-slow lately, taking 4, 6 and even 8 weeks. One of my letters was from Marguerite written 31st Dec. Wishing me a Happy New Year; one was a Valentine from Angie; two were Birthday cards! I enjoyed the cornucopia of greetings and savored the message in each letter!

Yesterday was also the last day of teaching this term. Exams began today and will continue through next week. In addition to correcting exams and preparing the final grades, I'll be going up to Malumfashi in Katsina State to give a couple of talks to help the folks celebrate Laity Week. I'm also going to have a mini-retreat for the girls at FGGC next door (Federal Gov't Girls College, a secondary school with grades 7, 8 + 9 so far), on the week-end.

My plan is to fly down to Akwa Ibom via P.H. sometime during Holy Week and stay until Easter Tuesday. Our Easter Holidays are cut short. The Ministry of Education has decided to change the school year back to the October-July schedule (from a January-November one). To do it means we lose a term. For the students in grades 9 + 12, who have to take a national exam, this is very tough, but it is tough all the way round for everybody. So, the seminary is dealing with the problem by cutting off 2 weeks of Easter holidays. We will probably have extra evening classes as well, and come July, we may lose more holiday time. Life is not dull.

Back in January, when life seemed a bit regular and routine, I decided to make some purple accessories for the church and chapel for Lent – tabernacle veils, altar and lectern hangings. the Rector let me buy some lovely Oken cloth which is basically a hand-woven, somewhat heavy cloth made in strips about 2 yards long and 1/2 yard wide. The one I bought was white with a design of purple and gold, with small openings adding a further design. I did manage to finish most of what I intended, though not all in time for Ash Wednesday. In early February, the unplanned events began happening.

On Feb. 8th, I was getting dressed when I heard the 6:45 rising bell, – followed almost immediately by shouts of the boys' voices. I wondered what it might mean – did someone see a snake? – was there an accident? In no time, I heard feet running across the compound toward the Father's house, then someone banging Father's door and calling him. He answered, and the boys gave the report loud and clear "Fire, Father, fire!" I looked out the window but saw nothing in the morning darkness. Water had been especially scarce the past 2 weeks, so I felt anxious and quickly finished dressing. Well, the fire, in the ceiling of one classroom, was out in 20 minutes if not less. Some of these boys experienced the burning of the school in 1987, so I thanked God we did not have a repeat of that. Rather, this incident took another twist.

On returning to the house, the Rector was told the kitchen had been burgled! – 2 gas stoves, a kerosene stove and some food thermoses. Were they, the fire and burglary, connected? Were there Muslims retaliating because of the Gulf War? Father called our electrician who saw there was no fault with any wires in the ceiling, but he found the remains of a burnt blanket that had been soaked in kerosene.

About 9 in the morning, I was called from class to join a small group of staff in the Rector's office. We were given all this info and asked to investigate. A good chunk of the next 2 school days were spent interviewing the night guards, the kitchen staff (on duty by 5 a.m.), the students who first saw the fire, any disgruntled students, other laborers, all to no avail. We did get back one gas stove, but we and the police resolved nothing.

Somehow, I never caught up with myself after that. The harder I tried the more I slid behind. The best laid plans...!

Early this term I volunteered to help out in the health area. My extra-curriculars were all outside the school, so I felt I should get involved a bit more. That decision has led to a really busy involvement. The little committee that was formed has done a lot, though lack of funds prevents us from doing all we would like. You would be interested to know the "regular" sicknesses – malaria, dysentery, worms, eye infections (from the dust), nose bleeds (from the very dry air), coughs, and colds. We've had several cases of typhoid, 3 of bilharzia, one of meningitis, one of hepatitis. We have our share of broken bones and sprains. Since we began, Father has hired a P.E. teacher who is who is an R.N. Unfortunately, he doesn't live on the compound. So I am the nurse/surrogate mother for anyone feeling bad. For X-rays, blood or urine tests, and anything the nurse can't figure out, I go up to Samaru with the students to a clinic. Some weeks I make that trip almost everyday. We had Niger Optical come and examine those with eye complaints. Little by little, we are organizing ourselves! And I'm learning the students names ever so much faster!

The homogeneous group of the math classes is going well. We would do better if we could have 3 or more groups with smaller numbers, but .... Success is also hampered by kids being out chunks of time for sickness or going home for school fees. Sometimes when the teacher of math III A isn't in, the kids will come into my room. However, the smart kids have their hands up to go to the board and are calling out answers to questions much faster than my B group, so my own students don't like them to come in. When I say "B-group only today please," my students are happy!

Other than my trips to Samaru to the clinic, I haven't travelled much. We had a Sisters Area Conference Meeting in Rigasa, Kaduna, and I went up to Gusau one Sunday to see the Dominican sisters and get my overnight bag which I had left in their car! (coming back from the Area Meeting)

I read a really good book by Carol Gilligan – *In A Different Voice*, and I'm halfway through *Biko* by Donald Woods. I'm still using Hildegard of Bengin for meditation – she would love today's rain and all its "greening" powers! I try hard with the periodicals to keep up with the world.

So life is busy and my hands are full. All is well in spite of fires and thefts and sickness. The Church is strong and growing – with a special mission here in northern Nigeria. It is great to be a part of it!

With lots of love and prayers for all,
Florence

Letter Twelve

25 April 1991

Dear Family and Friends,

Sannu to each of you! I pray you are well and enjoying the promise of springtime wherever you are! We have only had a few rains here, but each one brings the great flowering trees to greater beauty. The brilliant "flame of the forest" is everywhere, and many are magnificent. But the sun is hot. I remember often that we are near the desert. Shade is blessed coolness!

Here at the Seminary, we all moved from the pressures of the term's end, exams, grades, and filling report sheets into Holy Week celebrations without pause. In fact, I put my last entrees on the grade sheets Easter Monday! Contrary to my original plans, I left for Akwa Ibom on Easter Wednesday. Flexibility is a key word here. I flew down this time, by way of Lagos. I met Fr. Gaul Okon at the Lagos airport, also flying to Calabar, so I was able to sponge a ride with him up to Uyo. – one of the priests had come to meet him.

My stay in Akwa Ibom was short but sweet. I missed seeing the postulants who were on Easter break, but enjoyed my time with the Sisters. I stayed a few nights in Uyo and a few in Ikot Etuk Udo – and the week was over. I flew back on a direct flight from Port Harcourt to Kaduna. The plane was a small propeller plane that made a stop in Enugu and in Abuja before landing in Kaduna.

"Kada" is the Hausa word for "crocodile"; the plural, "kaduna" means "crocodiles." I haven't seen any myself, but they must have been here. Kaduna city was built at the junction of the Niger and the Benue Rivers very early in this century for the purpose of administering British rule over their newly conquered territory. No doubt, there were, and may still be, crocodiles in those rivers.

After returning from Akwa Ibom, I had a day's grace before joining the Vocation Team of Reverend Sisters for our trip to Kano for a short Vacation Rally. We came from Kano directly to Zaria and repeated our presentation. Flexibility was the key throughout, as the communications sent out were garbled when relayed verbally at the other end! Luckily, the sisters were good natured and compatible. We managed to find a spot for our posters, etc., and shared what we were able to in our little program. That was the weekend of April 12-14. We did a repeat performance in Kaduna on Wednesday the 17th. On the next weekend, we travelled south to Saminaka and Zonkwa, in Kaduna State, still.

Eugenia and Martin flew up on the Concord propeller plane on Friday the 19th to join us for the final weekend. This was the first time since I have been up here that anyone from Akwa Ibom has come up, so I was very excited! They were just great joining in our little band and "managing" with whatever! We stayed at the Social Center. They had no light in their bathroom; the restaurant ran out of food, so we had fried eggs and bread for supper – at the same price as a full meal; then left at 5:30 a.m. to begin the journey to Saminaka. When we arrived, we found that the parish priest had expected us the day before. It is a very rural area, so he was unable to get any young people together. He showed us a video, fed us, and packed us on to Zonkwa. There, we had a little more control of things, but found that everything we said in English had to be translated into Hausa. Our little program took 3 hrs. plus! In spite of all the unknowns, we all had a great time and the bond that grew among the sisters was beautiful. (The other sisters from Kaduna Archdiocese are all Nigerian and at least 20 years my junior!)

The Archbishop, who lent me his car and driver to meet Eugenia and Martin at the airport, also let us have them to get from Kaduna to Zaria on Sunday night. We joined Liz and Harry for their Sunday evening buffet – a gourmet's delight every time!

The 2 sisters slept there and joined me at the seminary on Monday. Nigerians delight in welcoming guests, and the staff and boys here are no different. Eugenia taught them a song with sign language which they thought was terrific! We had a quick look-round the seminary and Zaria and headed for the airport with no time to spare. So, of course, the car died on the way! Adomu, our driver, tinkered for 5 or 10 minutes under the hood while we held our breath. Although he got the car to start, he was all for turning back to get the pick-up for the journey. We were a united front – NO! There was no time to go back and still make the plane – so we went forward saying our traveling prayer. We made it to the airport with 10 minutes to spare!

That visit is like a dream, come and gone now! Classes have resumed and I've shifted my gears to the schedule and activities of the school term. However, I know the sister will come again, and I know the others will come too. This part of the country is a very important part of the Nigerian Church, and for that reason, I believe it will be part of SSND history. The Church is like the savannah lands – on the edge of the desert, dry and dusty and hot, but with a wonderful "greening power." The huge, bountiful mango trees are so prolific up here, the farmlands so vast, the flowering trees so beautiful, you can only marvel at what God can do, even on the edge of the desert! The predominant Muslim presence is a challenge, and in many specific incidents, an obstacle to the church, but the rains are coming. God's Spirit is moving in this place, and no one can doubt it.

As I write my class lists, I'm getting used to the names. We have Musa (Moses), Yakufu (Jacob/James), Yusuf (Joseph) and Isaac, Nehemiah, Micah, Hosea, etc. We have family names of Afuwai, Katuka, Tiokpat, Magari, Yamai, Jagaba, Iyaji, etc., etc.. I don't know every boys name yet, but I'm getting there. They are used to having me around now – the novelty has worn off, thank God. We are moving into a tough term – 2 terms are being squeezed into one, as they change the school year back to the Fall/Spring pattern.

28 April 1991

There have been riots in Katsina – Muslims burned down a Newspaper Office Building. These are Shi'ites, like those in Iran. Last week they came to Zaria to gather sympathy through a demonstration, to be held this past Friday. The Federal Gov't was very firm throughout the Gulf War about no demonstrations. These Shi'ites say they don't recognize the gov't – only Allah, so they went to the Emir in Zaria for permission to demonstrate. The Emir sent them to the Governor of Kaduna and then phoned the Gov. that they were coming. (These same Shi'ites had embarrassed the Emir in their mosque a few weeks earlier by throwing stones at him!) The Governor put the army on alert with the order to shoot to kill any demonstrators who arrived at his gate. No one arrived! On Friday, while the Muslims were at prayer in their mosques, some of the Shi'ites entered the market and harassed the market women, who would all be non-Muslims, of course.

The Emir called the priests and ministers to his palace on Friday morning to beg them to ask their people for peace if the fanatical Muslims started anything. Thank God there was no serious incident! In Bauchi State there were demonstrations and people were killed. Our own Governor of Kaduna is a Muslim, so clearly it is only a small group looking for trouble. I guess they feel their security threatened by events taking place in the world and are lashing out, like a scared kid or threatened animal. Do continue to pray for peace!

With love and prayers,
Gabriel

Letter Thirteen

11 June 1991

Dear Ange,

Hi, dear friend! How are you? I was so happy to hear from you how well things are going for you and Mike and how promising life has become. I am so delighted for you! I admire you and Mike tremendously for your search and struggle for an authentic love in your relationship – you couldn't do what you are doing if there wasn't lots of love already there. Please give my greetings to Mike.

Sister Virginia came up from Akwa Ibom for the weekend about 3 weeks ago. We really enjoyed ourselves. Then last week, Sister Sharon came over from the States to teach a course in television at the Catholic Media Center in Kaduna. After meeting her at the airport in Kano and settling her in at Kaduna, I went back this past weekend to be sure all was well – which it was. It was been nice to have kindred feminine spirits to talk to!

School is a bit chaotic and frustrating, but I keep plugging along. There are 3 other young women on the staff now and I'm trying to enlist them in some of my endeavors to bring a feminine influence to the school. I think there is some potential there.

I'm pretty O.K. except for a very difficult meeting which I went to last night. It's still very fresh in my mind, and I know the issue isn't finished – so I'm not at ease today. However, I suppose time will heal a great deal of it. It is so good to know I have a loving and faithful friend in you, Ange, who believes in me and loves me as you do! I praise and thank God for you! Do continue to write – I count on your encouragement and care!

Lots of love,
Gabe

Letter Fourteen

7 July 1991

Dear Family and Friends,

Sannuku! My greetings to all of you! It has been long since I've written, but it is not because you are out of my thoughts. I remember you often and keep you in my prayers as well.

Since my last letter, the time has just flown by me. S. Virginia Brien came up for a weekend, then S. Sharon Dei arrived. I met Sharon in Kano and we spent the night with the St. Louis Sisters there. The next day we travelled to Kaduna via Zaria and Sharon settled right in. Every weekend except one, I've been down to visit with her to try to see a bit of Kaduna. One weekend we had a wonderful journey to Makurdi in Benue State and saw Grace Anebi, our postulant, who was preparing for her exams. It has been grand to have SSND company. And Sharon fits in so perfectly, I'm optimistic she will come back next year.

In just a little more than 2 weeks, Marguerite will be here with Elaine Weber. A flexible plan is in place for her to experience Zaria and Kaduna and meet some of the people who have been very supportive of our SSND presence here. I'll be flying to Lagos to meet Marg and Elaine on the 22nd.

The anticipated frustrations of school are being fully felt as we come close to exams. Not only do we have 2 terms in 1, but we had additional interruptions because some of the Form IV (sophomore) boys tried to stage a riot. The Rector managed to nip it in the bud, thank God, but it took time to identify the instigators and decide how to handle the situation. About 12 boys have been expelled.

The homogeneous grouping in the junior math classes has been very successful. The math teachers will be very unhappy if we don't continue with it.

The Health Committee, another of my pet projects has also made progress in various areas of the student life. It has also kept me very busy!

The Archbishop has been trying to find a car for me to use. There is a 504 Peugeot that is in for repairs, but it is taking long. Last week he asked if I could manage a little Volks, but as it turned out, the battery is very weak. However, it may be fit to drive very soon and that will be nice, indeed!

It is hard to believe, but prices are still going up here. I don't know how people manage. Theft is a problem – one among many. But people struggle along and keep their spirits up. They are really great!

We are moving well into the rainy season, though it is not nearly so heavy as in Akwa Ibom. There are myriad shades of green everywhere. The trip to Makurdi, especially the piece through Plateau State, was gorgeous. It reminded Sharon and me of western Maryland!

Sharon and I both saw Makurdi as a marvelous place for SSND to plant itself. The Bishop had travelled, but the Vicar and the Dean asked me to come back in August and stay a bit longer, when the Bishop is there. The Diocese of Makurdi will probably be divided soon, with Otukpo as the new diocese.

This coming weekend, Sharon is coming to Zaria with 2 students to video the seminary here. I do hope it turns out well. If she takes the videos that her students are making home, it will be great. Hopefully, it will make our experiences here more vivid for you there!

Our students LOVE video. The rector is very generous about letting them use his own T.V. and Liz and Harry have a "lending library" of videos. One of their favorites is THE GODS MUST BE CRAZY. There is a sequel to that now, and they like that one just as much. I've never heard them laugh so much as at those two! I only wish I had access to some of the documentaries or educational films that are there in the States.

If I could do something to inject some greater interest in the students improving their English, I would be very happy. Spoken English is poor and written English is shocking. Since I don't really speak anything but my mother tongue, it seems foolish for me to criticize, except that English is the national language here and it is really essential for education and communication.

This letter has been interrupted several times and I'm anxious to get it in the mail. I did want to let everyone know that I am alive and well. Life is busy but pleasantly so and challengingly so. I know that the next few weeks are going to be very busy as well. I will be flying to Akwa Ibom with Marg on July 29th – the day final exams begin. After our meetings with the other sisters, I'll come back to correct exams and finish my grades. It will be mid-August before I have chance to write again.

So I wish you all well! Happy Birthday to all the Roeders who celebrate this month!! And many thanks to those who take time to drop me a line and keeps me up on news from that side!

With love and prayers,
Gabriel

Letter Fifteen

9 July 1991

Dear Lois and Carolyn,

Hi! How are you? I hope you are both well, and Joe, too.

Ruth tells me you've been a great help to her in caring for Daddy, so I know you've been busy. Going back and forth can't be easy. Thanks so much for all you are doing for all of us!

Elizabeth is finally out of the hospital – one year later! I still haven't seen her since I'm here. She needs a crutch to walk.

Please give greetings to everyone for me.

Lots of love,
Florence

Letter Sixteen

23 July 1991

Dear Angie,

Hi, Friend! Thanks so much for your lovely and loving letter! What good news it carried! I am so very happy for you and Mike! I just praise and thank God for your honesty and courage. You certainly have been so TRUE in your love for Mike. I pray your kids learn <u>much</u> from all that has transpired!

Life has been busy, as usual. S. Sharon Dei is here teaching television at the Catholic Media Center in Kaduna. My weekends are spent with her because I want her to have a good experience – which she surely has. She just LOVES the students (about 20 of them) and they love her. She is very warm and motherly, as well as an excellent, organized teacher and very competent in her field. Fr. McFarland said she has re-vitalized what was a dying program! She has been invited to come back next year, and she wants to do that. She would love to come to stay, but she is an only child and her mother would be alone.

My superior, S. Marguerite, is coming in tonight, so I am in Lagos waiting for her. She wrote that there is a possibility I may be recalled to Akwa Ibom temporarily, but I am hoping that will not happen. I've tried to plan a good visit up in Kaduna/Zaria before we go to Akwa Ibom for our meetings. Some very far-reaching decisions will have to come out of those meetings!

We have a small, furnished house (free) available, the promise of teaching posts at the Minor Seminary, and a dilapidated Volks to transport us. Everything is being served to us on a silver platter! I just hope it will impress Marg, along with the great needs of the Church up here! So, keep us in prayer!

S. Sharon has lots of videos from her students' assignments which I'm hoping she will take home and edit. It would be a wonderful view of life up here. If she does that, I'm sure I could get a copy for family and friends!

Well, Ange, give my love to Mike and the kids, to the gals in the Study Group, and any others. Stay as beautiful as you are!!

Lots of love,
Gabe

Letter Seventeen

1 August 1991

Dear Lois, Carolyn and Joe,

Hi! I hope you are all doing well. I received Lois' letter with news of each one and I was happy that everything is moving along – only her problem with grants was creating a snag.

I am down in Akwa Ibom with everyone. We will begin our meetings together this afternoon. Marguerite came up to Zaria first, and we had a really profitable tour of that area. Everyone was very positive and supportive about my presence there and the hope for more sisters to come. We also have encouragement to move into Abuja, Makurdi and Kaduna. We shall see...

The novices will be coming back in January for a 6 mos. apostolic experience—and we really do not have enough bodies to create communities for them. In order to accommodate them, I'm moving my home-visit forward to September so I will be back by December. Then I can get myself settled into the small house at A.B.U. campus that I'll be living in (it's the Catholic chaplaincy). The Archbishop also gave me a Volks and the rector assured me that if novices join me in Zaria, there will be teaching posts for them in the seminary. So, I am asking for 2 novices to come up. I hope it will be approved.

S. Sharon Dei flies home tonight via Kano. She had a marvelous time here. She taught a course in television as part of the summer program at the Catholic Media Center in Kaduna during June and July. She LOVED the students, the weather, the accommodations, the whole scene. And the students LOVED her. She knows her stuff and has always been a good teacher and a very motherly presence. She will be back next summer!

Thanks so much for the pictures – you've really gotten in some nice excursions. I'm glad. Thanks, too, for the generous gifts of money for me and for Elizabeth. Please thank Judy Lovechik, too.

I finally saw Elizabeth. She hobbles or uses a cane, but otherwise is her old self. She is crocheting caps and was happy for some wool which Dorothy Hunt had given me. Fidelis Akpan, Felicia Essien's in-law, is active in St. Vincent de Paul Society and has been very helpful with her. He is the one who holds her money.

Well, it won't be too long till I'm home. Please greet everyone for me. Take care –

Love,
Florence

Letter Eighteen

Dominican Convent
Yelwa, Sokoto State
16 August 1991

Dear Family and Friends,

Sannuku! It has been long since I written. I hope you everyone is well and enjoying whatever activities you are involved in. All is well here. I am with S. Rita in Yelwa for a few days vacation. Yelwa is on the Niger River, just north of Kainje Dam in northwestern Nigeria.

Because we are at the peak of the rains, everything is gorgeously green! There are fields of maize, rice, guinea corn, millet, though some of the maize was spoiled by too much rain. I'm told the soil is poor from being overused. After 5 yrs. use, it needs 15 to be fallow; if a tractor is used on it, it needs 50 yrs. That isn't evident to the eye of a novice. Sister Terry works in Development for Sokoto Diocese and works with some farming cooperatives, so she's full of interesting farming information. (She is from Kansas farm country, as well!)

There are seven tribes in the area, most of whom are Muslim. Those who are not were discriminated against with heavier taxes, no schools or clinics, etc. Now, with the establishment of local governments, that has changed, but they are very underdeveloped and very resistant to change. The women in one tribe wear only a mini-skirt (wrapper). Their bodies are tattooed everywhere and they have small pieces of bone jewelry in their lower lip and through their nose. We went to the market yesterday and saw all seven of the tribes mingling—very colorful, indeed! The market is located along the shore of the Niger, so it is very picturesque. It was also VERY hot and a bit humid.

Terri speaks of a few of these tribes as pre-literate. Her work with them has been slow and tedious, but she sees signs of hope here and there. Most of these people follow their African Traditional Religion. Some became Muslim under the economic pressure exerted on them and a few have become Christian.

S. Marguerite's visit was like a whirlwind. We were able to go to several places and meet many people. We went from Lagos to Kaduna to Zaria, to Abuja before going to Akwa Ibom. I'm sure it added a new chapter to her memories of Nigeria. During that visit it was decided that I would move my home-leave forward to September, and also that I would definitely move out of the Father's house at the seminary into the Catholic Chaplaincy on A.B.U. campus, a small, comfortable house with 2 bedrooms. We are requesting that 2 novices join me in January when they are on apostolic experience. As a single sister, I may not provide the ideal type of community for them, but it will be realistic and typical of their future here in Nigeria. It is a great heartache and a real poverty that other mature professed do not come out to join us in the work of on-going formation. However, we are called to risk in faith, so we continue along the road that brought us thus far, and trust that God is working harder and more effectively than we are! After all, it is his work and his kingdom we're building.

There has been a lot of sickness around this year. Malaria was very bad, typhoid is still around, and now bad outbreaks of cholera. Of course, it is the poor and undernourished who get sick. Government has MUCH to do in providing clean water for all, health education and health services. General education is also very wanting. But in the midst of struggle, these people are still filled with hope, laughter and song!

With love and prayers,
Florence

P.S. I forgot to mention the good news that I do have a little Volks. The shake, rattle and roll on the rough roads initially made me expect it to come apart momentarily, but so far it is still intact. It has been a few faults, but we're ironing them out a few at a time. I'm told the engine is good, so I will have faith. The little grey mare ain't what she used to be, but she gets me around Zaria and from here to Kaduna. What more could I ask?!

Letter Nineteen

27 August 1991

Dear Dot,

Hi! Surprise?! My good intention of writing to different people in our Group every so often didn't go so far. The road to hell etc. etc.!!

How are you? And how is your family? Thanks for including me on your Christmas list and giving me an update on each one. I hope by now your knee injury has healed. This last letter made me aware of how important music is to your whole family. That is really great – a wonderful thing to share! And you have such a nice family!

I'm glad you are all still enjoying Julian, I've been into Hildegarde of Bingen, who is another marvelous women. Besides writing, she painted, composed music and practiced herbal medicine!

By the time this reaches you, I may already be in the States. I've moved my home leave forward and I should be in Baltimore on September 11th. The reason for the change is that I'll be back here before January, when our novices go on 6 mos. apostolic experience. We don't have enough houses to receive them (they are 5 in number), so some may be stationed in Ghana. I'm requesting that 2 come up here.

When I return from home-leave I'll be moving into a small house on the University Campus – the Catholic Chaplain's quarters. The Catholic priest there is a lecturer, so he has staff quarters. The house is small and cute. I also have a little Volks now for getting back and forth to school.

We are still getting plenty of rain here. One priest said after seeing all this rain disappear into the earth, the story of Noah must be a fairy tale! It has rained 40 days and 40 nights and there certainly isn't enough water to carry any ark to the top of a mountain! Of course, it never rains all day or all night here, but it has been raining every day for a while. Then the sun comes out and dries it all up.

Dot, take care! Greet your family and our mutual friends!

With love and prayers,
Gabe

Letter Twenty

P.O. Box 338 A.B.U.
Zaria – Samaru
Kaduna, Nigeria
26 January 1992

Dear Family and Friends,

Sannuku! It has been more than a month since I left the States, and by the time this reaches you, it will be two months. So I had best get on the ball, or I will never remember all that has been happening.

After I left, I stopped for a few days in Germany to visit Bruce Roeder, my nephew, M'Young, and the children. It was cold and foggy, but we had a lovely visit all the same. We talked, toured and shopped. I'm really happy to have met Sharon for the first time, and to share a little time and space with all of them. M'Young – gave me a beautiful purple scarf from Czechoslovakia, and each time I put it around me on the cool harmattan mornings, it brings back all the pleasant memories of my stay with them.

I arrived in Kano on schedule. The harmattan was and still is quite pleasant with its dusty haze and periodic cold. It dropped into the 50s at night, but I was told it had been much colder prior to my coming. Some of the nomadic people on the Jos plateau had died from the cold. Some people are saying it is the worst ever, but I remember hearing similar stories about 10 years ago.

There was a petrol shortage all through the northern part of the country, and that which was available was very costly. So, of course, the price of transport went up-just when Christians wanted to travel to their homes for the Christmas holidays. The taxis were not stopping at Zaria so I stayed in Kano a day and a half hoping to get a ride but in the end I had to "charter" a taxi, i.e., take it by myself but pay for a full load of passengers. This petrol problem followed me to Akwa Ibom and back. Generally speaking, it has finished, but now and again it shows its ugly head. Yesterday I sat in line at the petrol station for an hour to get gas so I could travel to Kaduna.

When I arrived in Zaria I found my room smothered in dust. Musa and I washed the floor and wiped everything before I could settle in. By the next day there was already a new sheen of dust. For the next few days I greeted people, tried to reorganize myself to get to Akwa Ibom, and find out if the planes were flying to Port Harcourt. That news wasn't good so on Christmas day I took advantage of a ride as far as Kaduna to check further on the planes. On Friday, I eventually got a plane that had to fly back up to Kano to get enough fuel to reach Lagos; from there we went to Enugu and then to Port Harcoourt. Jesus spent a lot of time traveling—on foot—so maybe all of this is good for me?

I finally arrived at Ikot Etuk Udo, just a few hours late for our Area meeting. We had a good few days together. From there I went to our convent in Uyo where I made my retreat. It was good to see all the SSNDs and catch up on news. I thought I would see the second year novices but was only able to see Theresa, who was staying on in Ikot Etuk Udo. That was real disappointment, however, there was a special treat in store for me – Martin agreed to come back to Zaria with me.

The journey back was more of the same, so I won't bother to recount it all. Martin thinks I am just bad luck! Anyway we had a great 10 days together. She helped me try to get the house at A.B.U. ready to "pack in." Actually, we thought we WERE going to pack in, but the dust, dirt and confusion we found changed that idea. It seemed like every drawer, closet and cupboard were loaded with papers, files, books, etc. that were soaked with dust t and belonged to a Priest who used to live there about five years ago. This got sorted and carried to garage, and then we began to clean. The more we cleaned, the more we saw that needed cleaning: So, we just kept at it, but alternated the work with a bit of relaxation. We shopped, ate at the Emanto Restaurant, had a guided tour of Kano, a nice visit with the St. Louis with the St. Louis Sisters, and dinner with Liz and Harry., on the two Sundays.

Martin has gone back to Akwa Ibom, and I am finally living in the new house – still chasing dust which comes in through the louver windows that will not close tightly. I remember that it took me 3 months to get my little room in the Father's House clean to my satisfaction, so I guess it will take at least that long. There are several orange trees in the yard, and they are in blossom right now. The fragrance is a lovely treat. There is also a mango tree, some banana trees, paupua trees, some grape vines. Tomatoes and lettuce have been planted (for me) by a gardener who comes for an hour or so each day. He is employed by the Catholic Parish near the campus here. Harmattan lilies were in bloom when I first moved in, and there are a few cactus here. Surprisingly, the soil is a beautiful, rich, black soil.

There is a young Franciscan Sister staying with me while she tries to get accommodation in the hostels. She has been great helping with the cleaning, and she is pleasant company for me. Yesterday, I met several other Americans at a party in the American Consulate in Kaduna. You can never be wanting for friends or interesting People here!

The Volks has a new coat of grey paint, and it runs, but it is, without a doubt, an old lady. It is a great blessing to have it to get from here to the Seminary on school days and to do my shopping. For trips outside Zaria, I borrow the Rector's car.

Classes began last Wednesday at the seminary, and I'm teaching 21 periods of math. Those first few days exhausted me, so I am glad for this day of rest. I'm way behind in everything, but that is more usual than not – hopefully, this letter will make up for my lack of writing!

There is a bird outside that sounds the same note just like a dripping faucet – a drop of music. I wish I could see it.

My best wishes to all those whose birthdays I've missed! I pray everyone is well. Be assured that I am doing fine. Please give my greetings to all,

With love and prayers,
Gabriel (Florence)

Letter Twenty-one

27 February 1992

Dear Lois and Carolyn,

Hi! How are you both? I hope all is well. Enclosed is a letter from Elizabeth that was sent to L.M. Roeder at the Motherhouse. It was given to S. Virginia who carried it back here and sent it along with Anne Vogel, who came up for a visit last weekend. So it has travelled!

I heard that Carolyn has some lumps in her breast. How did tests turn out, Carolyn? I'm anxious to hear. I surely do hope everything is O.K.

I've tried my "glare glasses when driving at night, but I'm still not comfortable. The lights (headlights) of my car are at least partly at fault. However, I had them fixed once and am reluctant to put out more money for bulbs that don't last. The only time I go out at night is on Sunday when I go over to Liz and Harry's for supper and video, and Fr. McGovern usually goes too. He is here in Samaru, so he takes me.

My little house is nice, but dreadfully dusty all the time because of the harmattan. It needs sprucing up in many areas, but I'm still waiting for the carpenter and mason to come do some basic patch jobs. After that, maybe paint or new curtains that fit!

I hope you will share my letter with Joe and give him my love. All, take care. Greetings to anyone I know!

Lots of love,
Florence

Letter Twenty-two

F.O. Box 338
Ahmada Bello University
Samaru – Zaria, Kaduna
3 May 1992

Dear Family and Friends,

My greetings to everyone: I pray you are all well and that your Easter was a happy and joy-full one.

Life here seems to be packed like a Dagwood sandwich – full and overflowing with rich and wonderful things, but too much to fit between my teeth. Deadlines seem to guide me through the maze of activities and choices.

Harmattan has mostly gone, though we still have a few traces now and again. Hot, HOT weather has come. I have a thermometer inside the house which used to read 80° most days. When it began to read 90° on most days, I decided to take it outside in the sun. It quickly rose to the maximum reading of 120° – and could go no further! It got hotter still after that. Hair and bra were wet always!

We have now had two rains, each of which cooled everything off. And now people are busy planting or preparing the ground for planting.

The economic situation here, unbelievably, has gotten worse and worse. Prices are uncontrollable. Many things have increased 100% and more. Many people can no longer afford margarine OR bread, eggs or milk. They are luxuries. A gallon of engine oil is N100, which is like $100. Even a professor's salary here at Ahmadu Bello University doesn't allow the person to buy a car anymore – or even a motorcycle for that matter. Every car owner has to patch, patch, patch. And to add to the circus, the market is full of fake products. Hospitals are getting bare, schools are looking dilapidated, and streets are getting crowded with beggars. But the rich are getting richer-and that seems to be the measure of progress.

My neighbors who share the other half of the house I live in are Moslems – one man, two wives, 5 children, and some other extended family members. The wives only seem to come out to go to market, but they are friendly, and the children are very friendly. The man of the house doesn't seem to be home much, but he has come over to borrow things after which the children bring me some nice thing to eat.

My little house is in much better shape, but still hard to keep clean. The Sisters were up from Akwa Ibom for our Area Meeting and they enjoyed seeing the progress. The big news is that I'll be leaving the house in August. Sr. Sharon Dei and I will be going to Jos to teach in the Major Seminary. It is an exciting move and Jos is the most favored city climate-wise among the expatriates. However, I'll be leaving not only Zaria, but the Kaduna Archdiocese and many people who have been kind and caring and sometime extraordinarily generous to me. I shall miss them sorely!

The trees on my compound are bearing fruit and many flowering trees are in their splendor. The Flame of the Forest put out its gorgeous red carpet branches to welcome the Sisters from Akwa Ibom – and you see them everywhere. The grape arbor is thick with leaves and gives a marvelous "cool" effect to the window at the back of the house. And the birds! Lovely to look at and lovely to hear!

Last week Sr. Virginia and I went to Makurdi Diocese. The Bishop there is inviting us into his diocese and wanted to show us the land he is offering us. We were in Marurdi, Gboko, Agagbe, Otukpo, Ankpa and Oba-Otukpa. We met wonderful people along the way, some we knew, and enjoyed the wonderful hospitality that is always characteristic here, no matter how tough life is. We saw the famous Benue River and the rice fields made possible by its flooding during the rainy season, we saw the foothills of the Jos Plateau, a beautiful scene of distant rolling hills from the landsite in Gboko. Makurdi is just about midway between Zaria and Uyo, so I hope to include a map for those interested. Makurdi is also reasonably close to lots of important places like Abuja, Enugu, Onitasha, Jos, Kaduna, etc.

There is lot of good news in the good people with whom I rub elbows day to day: – Father McFarland whose house is always open and who is ready to help out with his car, his driver, a meal; the Bowyers who lent us their house, van, driver, washerman, cook and housegirls for our Area Meeting and gave us money to entertain ourselves besides; Liz who is always there to solve a problem, find an electrician or carpenter, serve her wonderful Sunday buffet with a video to top off the evening; the priests who are so solicitous and helpful and eager for SSND to stay in Zaria! In spite of the bleak economy and the pain and shame it is, there is caring and sharing, singing and celebration. Everyone seems to be holding their breath until the elections take place that will remove them from military rule. By January, we should once again be a Republic with an elected President. We pray!

Once again, I send you greetings and wish you well. I'm grateful to those who write, even though I don't! THANKS!

With love and prayers,
Florence

Letter Twenty-three

6 May 1992

Dear Lois, Carolyn and Joe,

Hi! How is everyone? And everything? I do hope all is well!

I'm sorry this letter is so long in coming—I'm paving the road to hell with my good intentions, as usual!

Lois the books you sent arrived yesterday—and my own sacks the day before. I'm glad they arrived safely—thanks so much for sending them! Now if I just get the time to read them!! Would you believe I'm only half through the one on the Warrior Spirit?

School is resuming today; because of fees, many of the students have been sent home. Without money, the rector can't buy food. Prices are terrible and they get worse daily.

I wanted to ask you to put Nancy Burns on the list of those who get my letter, but I think I once suggested to Lois Schiaffino that she pass hers on. Maybe you could see if she is doing that? And I think I also added Jane Roeder. Padraig Flanagan is back in Ireland, so no need for his name on the list.

You've probably already heard of the move to Jos from Sharon. Many people say Jos is the nicest city, but it doesn't really strike me as all that different from the few times I've been there. I know it has gorgeous flowers and lots of cactus. People use cactus for fencing to keep the animals out of their farms. When I get there, maybe I'll see more. Patty is there, so that is really nice.

How was Jimmy's wedding? And the trip to Puerto Rico? I hope all went well!

Marg wrote that there are finally some more Sisters in Baltimore interested in coming—perhaps in 1993. Thank God! The Generalate is also asking for Sisters to go to Romania to help the Sisters get back on their feet after 40 yrs. of repression. One has gone to Hungary to help in teaching English. Our internationality is really a blessing.

I guess you know Marg did not accept nomination for re-election, so we'll be getting a new superior for Nigeria. Christine was re-elected as Provincial.

Please give greetings to all! Take care!!

Lots of love,
Florence

Letter Twenty-four

June 15, 1992

Dear Lois,

Peace and Joy to you! In March, I was called by the School School Sisters of Notre Dame to be one of the Provincial Councilors for the next four years. On June 21, Sister Christine Mulcahy – Provincial Leader, and Sisters Patricia McLaughlin, Joan Minella, Carleen Cekal, and myself – Provincial Councilors, will be prayerfully installed during Mass at the Motherhouse.

I have already been assigned as contact person to the Nigerian Missions and I am delighted to be able to get to know and learn of the work of the sisters there. If all goes well, I will be traveling to Nigeria on July 12, staying there until the 23rd, and then attending the SSND African Assembly in Ghana during the last week of July. I will be returning to the States on August 2.

I just wanted to introduce myself to you and to let you know I will be contacting you by phone from time to time. If there is anything I can do for you in the future, please feel free to write or call me. OFFICE: 377-5418 – HOME: 828-7504.

We will all miss Sister Marguerite Weiler. She will be leaving Baltimore at the end of the month and will be Pastoral Minister at St. Matthew Parish in Hallandale, Florida. How grateful all SSNDs are to her and I know how much the sisters in Nigeria will miss her presence among them.

With prayers,

Sister Joan

I'll be in touch before I go to Nigeria. It will be great seeing S. Gabriel again.

Letter Twenty-five

P. O. Box 338 A. B. U. Samaru – Zaria
8 July 1992

Dear Family and Friends,

Greetings to all: I hope you are all enjoying your summer as much as I am enjoying mine. The rains have brought the grass back, so everything is lush and green. It has a cooling and soothing effect on me, – like Melvin Avenue.

The recent riots in Kaduna city, Zaria and southern Kaduna State have been brought under control, but the calm and peace are only external. There is great anger, hurt and mistrust on every side. Many, many people were brutally killed. Almost anyone you talk to has a family member or a friend who was a victim. There is a LONG history of bad feelings between some of the tribes. Part of that is due to the British who put the peoples of southern Kaduna under the Emir of Zaria in the North for organizational purposes. There are ethnic, cultural and religious differences between the tribes in southern Kaduna and the Hausa and Fulani in the North. And now there is an accumulation of the stories of oppression, injustice and harassment at the hands of the Emir. Often the straw that ignites the blaze is over land or market space or other economic or financial matters, but in the end, it is usually looked back upon as the result of religious differences. The bloody riots of the past 5 or 10 years have never been resolved or reconciled to anyone's satisfaction.

There were some very tense days here in Zaria, with many people killed, but I was never near any of the violence. The Seminary stayed opened and functioned normally for the most part. Since then, many people have assured me that such things never happen in Jos. People are more peace-loving there, or perhaps of milder temperament in the milder climate. We shall see!

The A.B.U. is back in full swing – temporarily. After the students were called back after their protests, the teachers went on strike. A mediation board was set up, so they were required by law to return to the classroom for a month. They had been "mediating" for a year prior to the strike, so the future is anybody's guess. Because of the IMF, it is impossible to buy books and periodicals from outside the country, so libraries are hurting, and so, too, the students and teachers. Everybody's hurting – hospitals, businesses, secondary and primary schools, etc. Those who sell food seem to be the winners.

After 2 weeks of "running up and down" and making phone calls and sending FAXs to get visas to the U.S. for Sharon and three other Sisters who will be coming as visitors, I was body-stiff and seat sore from riding in taxis to Kaduna, Abuja and Jos, but there were SO MANY people who rallied round to help, that the experience was a very positive one. It is always an exercise in frustration to try to "make" things work, and a heavy lesson that I am not as patient a person as I like to think I am!

And now Sharon is here, already in full swing in her Television Course. Getting Sharon's 16 cartons and her extra luggage out of the cargo at the Kano airport took a week and lots more friends, but that is Sharon's story to tell. Her initiation was topped off with an attack of malaria! She got expert TLC from the staff at the Media Center and the OLA Sisters at St. Gerard's Hospital, and was back on her feet teaching as quick as a wink. I saw her today (9th) and she looks great, doing her thing in the T.V. studio.

I have been to Jos a few times to "encourage" things to fall into place. Getting some of my things up there, finding a good bank, getting a P.O. Box, finding a house and some other sundry things, require contacts and time and "running around." Nothing has actually settled into place properly yet because we still do not have a house. Since exams begin at the Seminary next week and I go to Ghana the week after, then to Akwa Ibom for another meeting, I can easily panic if I think too far into the future. Teaching at the Major Seminary begins the first week of September. Sharon has agreed to come to Jos next week to look at the house which seems most promising, if the Sem agrees to the rent. It is being renovated., so there will be cleaning up to do, furniture to buy, curtains to make, etc., etc.

Sharon will be leaving for the General Chapter in early October for about 6 weeks and then again at Christmas for a month or so. Maybe after that things will settle down and God will bless me with a little boredom and monotony! My friend Patty Wilson and her husband are in Jos and I am making new friends and trying hard to find my way around the town.

The rains are really here, and the world has turned so green! The rain brings mosquitos but it also cools things off. If there is a storm with the rain, NEPA (Nigerian Electric Power Authority) goes off too. I'm always happy to go to bed early and get some extra shut-eye!

Many thanks to everyone for letters, messages, prayers and good wishes!

With love and prayers,
Gabriel

Letter Twenty-six

20 July 1992

Dear Lois and Carolyn,

Hi! Thanks so much for your tape! What a nice treat! I'm sorry I missed the 1st one, but I certainly enjoyed this one.

Lois, right after I received the packages of books (I wrote to let you know), I received 2 more packages. I'm sure they are complete. Many thanks!

I'm enclosing a copy of my general letter. Sr. Kitty Malstrom is taking over from Sharon, but I'm afraid she might be on vacation or retreat since this is summer break there. I'm sending her one copy, but I'm also sending you and Ruth one each.

Robin Roeder sent me a lovely letter and a pack of pictures from the wedding. It must have been beautiful! I enjoyed seeing it even from a distance!

Tomorrow I go to Kaduna, then early Wednesday to Lagos. That evening to Ghana for a week and then to Uyo for a week or so. I'm anxious to settle in Jos in time to prepare my head for teaching. School starts the 1st week of September.

Sorry to be rushed! Please give my love to everyone!

Florence

▲ Ordination Day with seminarian Keyito Okake and
Sr. Sharon Dei, Jos, 1993

1992-1994

Moving Up Country

In September 1992, Gabe moved to Jos. Located southeast of Zaria and more central in the country, Jos is on the plateau and approximately 4,000 feet above sea-level. Something of a "melting-pot," Jos had in recent years seen clashes between Christians and Muslims. For two years, Gabe taught Scripture and theology at St. Augustine Major Seminary there. Both in Jos and earlier in Zaria, Gabe lived with Sr. Sharon Dei, an old friend with whom she had taught in the 1970s at St. Maria Goretti High School in Hagerstown, Maryland.

Letter Twenty-seven

St. Augustine Seminary P.O. Box 182 Jos
Plateau State, Nigeria
3 September 1992

Dear Family and Friends,

My greetings to each of you! From Tin City, finally. Jos, which is on a high plateau, has had tin mining going on for many years, hence its nickname, Tin City. We are at the peak of the rains, and it can get quite cool after – in the 50s or 60s. I need a sweater, but some people prefer a woolen scarf around their neck:

This is the place where roses and cactus grow together. Some of the cactus are in flower, and the roses are beautiful, – all kinds and colors. Some poinsettia are in bloom, too. Guava are plentiful right now, and corn is still around. You can buy fresh roasted corn along the road side when it is in season.

There are beautiful mountains (hills?) in the distance, if you are in a place where you can see them. It looks a bit like western Maryland. The skies are dramatic and beautiful in the rainy season, always changing as the clouds fill up, billowing across the blue. And the blue can be so blue, – washed clean!

I left Zaria finally on the 18th of August. That seems like years ago! Since then, I've been on the road a lot between Jos, Kaduna and Abuja, trying to get one more visa.. So far, I have not succeeded with this one. Sharon and I still have no house, so we are ,staying with the Holy Child Sisters at their Renewal Centre and Novitiate here in Jos. Their hospitality is just marvelous, and I am so grateful! The house we had our eyes on did not work out. It is in the same unfinished state now that it was in June.

Part of every day, sometimes all day, is spent in househunting. Diana, my mentor, and I follow any lead we are given. We look at the house, then try to find out who owns it, who holds the key, when we can see inside. Any one of these steps can take all morning. We are focusing on an area called Rock Haven, right on the Zaria Road as you come into Jos on the north end. It is near St. Marumba Catholic Church and a boys secondary school by the same name, and about a 5 minute drive from the seminary. In between the househunting, I try to move other things along, like P.O. Box, bank account, immigration transfer, etc., etc., etc.

Sharon is finishing up loose ends at the Media Centre in Kaduna. The seminarians are on retreat, so our classes will only begin next week, the 7th. We have finally been given offices at the seminary, though they hadn't found the key to my own yet. All my books are still in cartons in Sharon's office. (No desk or bookcases, yet.) We were given a nice 504 for our use, temporarily. The one we are supposed to have is a Passat, which is being repaired from an accident. Although I'm still getting to know my way around Jos, it is a big relief to be a little independent. The windshield wipers and the fuel gauge in the 504 do not work, but the engine is fine and the tires are good, so we thank God. Sharon and I had been thinking of investing in a camel and a tent with indoor plumbing, but now we can skip the camel!

Over the past month or so, I've had occasion to be at a few parties/celebrations. Of course, they are fun and entertaining, but I've been struck at how religious they are. I'm talking about ordinary lay folks, young people included. Often we begin with prayer. We sing religious songs and choruses and dance to the same. I think it must be a uniquely African experience that people are so happy and grateful to God for his goodness that they can't sit still: They really sing for joy because of what Jesus has done for us. And all of this is interspersed so simply and naturally with other songs, dance, sharing of food, stories, good wishes and congratulations: The gifts of the African church to the universal Church will surely be its dynamic, joy-filled faith. In spite of hard times and real suffering, their sense of relationship in community buoys them up. People take priority over things, time and money, hence the wonderful hospitality, even among the poor. Love knows no measure!

Our trip to Ghana was grand. The travel part was not without its mishaps, but the get together with friends and the meetings were great. Such gatherings of SSNDs are common in the States, but they are an uncommon treat here. After Ghana, we had our Area Meeting in Akwa Ibom and really accomplished a lot. I left immediately after with Mara Frundt, our SSND Cross Cultural Mission Coordinator. We journeyed to Kaduna via Lagos (UGH!) to visit Sharon and get a quick look-see at Zaria. Mara had been eager to see the North, but Zaria was a far as we could reach with the time we had. She did **see** the differences in dress and architecture in Zaria, but she very much wanted to see Kano, and also Jos, since that is where Sharon and I will be. Next time, Mara!

This letter is a bit rushed, but I hope it makes sense. I'm anxious to get it out before classes begin. I feel certain we are going to find a nice, suitable house soon, so you are all welcome to come and visit. Just ask at the SHCJ novitiate or at the seminary where we are.

As you leave your summer breaks behind, I wish you well in whatever lies ahead. Many, many thanks for the letters and gifts which you send. I am very, very grateful!

With love and prayers,
Gabriel

Letter Twenty-eight

31 October 1992

Dear Ange,

Hi! How are you? And how are Mike and the kids? Did you have a good trek to the west? I'm anxious to hear about it all!

I've had this aerogram addressed for weeks, but just couldn't get time to sit down and write. This weekend, I'm in Kaduna, trying to see a dentist who can do caps, so it has been a little break for me.

Sharon is in Rome for the General Chapter. She has been there about a month; she's due back on Nov. 11th. We are still living with the Holy Child Sisters in Jos—in their Novitiate. They are really so good to us! Our house is almost ready, but the "staff house" (boys quarters, it is called here!) is not ready. We want to hire a married couple to live there to help us with cooking, laundry, driving, etc.—and also be a security for us against theft while we are away during the day. It is a pity that theft is so rampant. We have a walled compound with a big gate, as do most of the houses in the area. It's like renting a cage in the zoo! However, not to complain, because we looked long before we found a suitable and convenient house. It looks like it will still be some weeks before we move in though!

School is fine. I enjoy the seminarians and staff and the teaching. In trying to get them to read more (in the absence of textbooks) in the library, I've gotten myself involved in a committee to improve the library. The librarian is the other member of the committee. It is a good library—nice building and many fine books for scripture and theology, but lack of funds for the past few years have made the library look a bit dowdy and current materials are lacking. We're trying to make it <u>look</u> attractive and inviting as well.

There are always the "extra curriculars" that keep me busy after school hours—going to the bank, immigration, getting the car repaired, shopping, etc., etc., etc. Just finding a dentist to fix my tooth has taken ever so many hours—and it still isn't finished! I'm also trying to get the seminarians involved with the 8 boys at the children's prison. The children are from about 6-16 yrs. old and they have no program at all. They sweep the grounds and do their laundry but have no classes or training at all. The seminary isn't all that far away, so the seminarians could do something.

In a couple of weeks, our first profession of Nigerian women will be held in Ghana. Immediately after, we will welcome them here in Nigeria, so I'll be travelling down to Akwa Ibom for the celebration, followed by an Area Meeting. When I get back to Jos, we will have just about 2 weeks to exams. Correction of papers is my most unfavorite part of teaching!

So, I'm alive and well, Ange, and very busy! Thanks so much for your letter. You are a beautiful and faithful friend! My love to you and to all.

Gabe

Letter Twenty-nine

Spring, 1993

Dear Family and Friends,

My greetings to each of you from Jos! I know it has been ages since I've written a decent letter, but I am still here, – alive and well. Even though there are political and economic problems in the country, we are managing to live very normal lives. We spend more time looking for petrol and more money in purchasing it, but we are still using the car.

Living in Jos is a very different experience from that of Zaria. For one thing, I'm back in community again, for which I'm very grateful. Sharon Dei, who is also teaching at the seminary where I'm teaching, and with whom 1 lived before, and Ngozi Udoye, one of our newly professed Nigerians who is teaching at St. Murumba Secondary School for boys, are my community members. After _many_ months of looking for a suitable house to live in, we finally found a lovely four-room house in an area very convenient to both of the schools we teach in. We are hoping for one of the newly professed from the next group of novices at the end of this year, so our house will be full!

I'm teaching major seminarians who are from the various dioceses in the northern part of Nigeria. The average class size seems to be around eighty. I can barely see the faces of the boys in the back of the room! If I meet them outside, I can't even recognize them. However, they are very friendly, concerned young men who are most gracious in overlooking our blunders! They have practically no textbooks, but there is a good library. Within the past 5 or 10 years, the library has been neglected because of the high cost of books, periodicals and newspapers, and the current books are fewer, but it is still good. And the boys are eager to learn. For the most part, I'm teaching within my field, which I enjoy. I did sweat through a semester of Church History and a semester of Theological Anthropol, I probably learned more than _they_ did! The daily schedule is a bit rigid, – not too unlike that at the minor seminary in Zaria. The boys love sports, especially soccer, music and drama. Their singing at Mass is always a real treat, no matter which of their many languages they sing in. And there are always some who excel in their native instruments, especially the drums, – the heartbeat of Africa!

The house we are renting is a new house, so various and sundry things didn't always work. It took a while to iron out the wrinkles, or at least figure out which one had their source in the house. Up until last month, water was a problem – it wasn't there! When the rains came we found that the roof leaked, we had no grass on the compound, so the rains began washing our topsoil away, etc., etc. We have lots of grass now, plus some young trees and many plants and flowers. By the time our lease is up in three years, the place will be beautiful!

Being in a new city meant learning my way around, which bank was good and where it was, where to find fresh vegetables, where to buy meat, where the main market was, where the Alien registration office was, how to register for a post office box. None of these is ever done in just one try, but I can find my way around the town without getting lost now, even if I don't always know the names of the streets. I found out that to have a bank account in the name of SSND, the congregation had to be registered at the Development Office at the State Secretariate. For over 12 months, I have been visiting that office and the process is still not complete! There are all kinds of such red-tape things that just gobble up my time (I'm the only driver, thus far). The only way to do all these things is to ask for help, so in the course of the year we've made many friends! The different expeditions usually make good stories as well!

Our house is very near the Sisters of the Holy Child Jesus novitiate and renewal center. In fact, Sharon and I lived there for about three months until our own house was ready. The sisters have been great friend to us. I taught a scripture class to the novices once a week in Prophets last semester which I enjoyed greatly. Anytime I am by myself, they always invite me up for meals or Mass or to join them for whatever is going on. Last month I had the opportunity to drive to Bauchi with them to visit their convent there. They took me on a tour to see the places that had been burned in the riots of last year! Wow! I also was fortunate in attending a Mass celebrated in the Zairean Rite which was a special treat. Liturgies in general are filled with lively music and song, sometimes some body rhythm, and processions, and are very participative, even during the homily. People love coming together to worship, and are seldom bored or sleeping.

We have an Augustinian monastery in Jos. The young men attend the seminary, so they are in our classes. As a result, we are always invited to their celebrations. Sometimes it is a Mass for vows, but sometimes it is purely social. It is always a good opportunity to meet other sisters and priests. To get to the monastery, you have to drive down a road which is actually part of the lumber market. It is in dreadful condition because of the heavy trucks which carry the lumber in, coupled with the heavy rains. It is a dirt road, so the people have put rocks down to prevent the cars from getting stuck. I think there is an ice cream called 'rocky road.' Well, let me tell you, the experience of driving on this road, especially right after or during a rain, is just like driving through rocky road chocolate ice cream! That the rocks don't tear your tires is amazing. It makes the potholes of other roads look tame! And all along one side of the road, on relatively dry ground, are people selling their various wares, looking like this is the most natural situation in the world.

Our house seems to be a beehive of hospitality, as our many friends drop by to see us or one of our priest friends comes for Mass and supper. We have a VCR that has been the source of much pleasure for us. Helene, our cook, housekeeper and laundress lives in a small "staff" house on our compound with her husband and two children. Sometimes her younger brother is there too to help her out. We also have a young man, a nephew to our landlord, living in a room in our staff house. He cuts our grass, cares for the flowers and does any of the heavy chores. These folks just love to watch video. Even though they may not catch all of the English, they seem fascinated. Sometimes a video may provide an opportunity for making them aware of other things. Such was the case with The King and I: we found Thailand on the map, talked about ice and snow, showed them England and Norway, etc. The same with Fiddler or The Sound of Music.

We've been especially busy this year with work to be done for SSND here in Nigeria. As we grow, we become more organized. We now have Area Meetings which usually last 4 days and are always packed with matters to be decided or discussed. God continues to bless us with fine young women who want to join us. There are about five up here in the "north" who come to visit, or to join us when we drive down to Akwa Ibom. We are all involved in one way or another in helping out with the Formation Program, even the newly professed. We are in need of more houses and areas of ministry for these people when they are professed, and all of that must be searched out and considered. While it is very demanding of our time, it is very, very exciting for us. We have come a long way since Mel first came in 1974! Our silver jubilee will be in 1999, by which time we will have some finally professed Nigerian SSNDs. We will certainly have more young women with us and more SSND convents and maybe an SSND – owned school. Invitations from the bishops are not lacking! And we have some ideas of our own, like a hostel for student sisters and a women's university. All God's works proceed slowly, but God is working overtime with us, believe me!

Jos is a lovely place to live. It seems to be the favorite spot for many people because of the cooler, drier climate. We are high on a plateau, with a view of mountains in the distance something like Middletown Valley in western Maryland. There are rocks all around! Piles and piles of rocks, in most unusual arrangements! You would think some giant had been playing with them for toys in some bygone era and just left them like that. Why they don't fall is amazing, though I'm told that sometimes they do. Because of the more temperate climate, there are familiar flowers, fruits and vegetables that grow, – like roses or strawberries or lettuce. We still have a rainy season and a dry season, and it can be quite cold at night or after a rain, probably because we are still close to the Sahara. And when it is cold, wool caps, sweaters, coats and mufflers are in! There are lots of wildflowers in addition to the many other flowers and flowering trees. There are poinsettias, cactus, and many whose names I don't even know.

If all goes according to plan, I will be home in the States for my home leave in the summer of 1994. School finishes in June or even May, so as soon as I have my 160+ exams corrected and my grades completed, I will leave. Our African Assembly will be held in Kenya in 1994, around the end of August, and I would love to come back by way of Kenya if I can. We have an Interprovincial Novitiate there for East Africa as well as the one in Ghana for West Africa. It will be a chance for me to see Maris Simon, Carola and other friends, and the African Assemblies are always exciting.

I send good wishes to all of you and apologize that I can't write individual letters. Be assured that all is well here and that I think of you and pray for you often.

With love and prayers,

Gabriel

Letter Thirty

4 July 1993

Dear Lois + Carolyn,

Hi! How are you? I received your letters via Chris and Joan, along with your gifts of money, books, and batteries. Thanks so much! Thanks, too, for the money for Elizabeth. In case I don't get time to write to Judy Lovechik, please thank her for me as well. I'll be writing her soon. Chris is leaving tomorrow, so I'm trying to get at least a letter or two ready. I'll send more with Joan later.

We've really enjoyed having our visitors here. The journey is a bit tough for them, but they'll have good stories to tell when they get back! We've been many places and met many people, all new to them, so I'm sure they'll be dizzy.

Joan is staying on till August 25th, and we're delighted about that! She'll be here with us in Jos until the 15th of July, and then she'll go back to Akwa Ibom. We have an Area Assembly in Uyo in August, so we'll see her again there.

I was happy to follow the developments with Terry. I'm sure, Carolyn, it's hard to think of not using Terry. Life is full of "transitions!" May all go well!

Lois, a trip to Nigeria sounds wonderful! I pray the political situation gets straightened out soon. At the moment, I doubt you would even get a visa! Our economic situation keeps falling as well – yet we are still counted the best off of most African countries!

Patty (Woods) Wilson should be home by now. She and her husband will be in Searcy, Arkansas with her parents until they find a house or apartment. I want to get a note off to her too, but... it's hard to control time here. She sent us a post card from the Ivory Coast and wrote from Tanzania.

There are a few trips still on the agenda for me, but in between I'll rest, try to squeeze in a retreat, catch up on mail, and start to prepare for classes in September. We have a petrol shortage – for what reason, we're not sure – and Jos is always the hardest hit. It means extra running around, extra money for black market prices of petrol, but thus far we've not had to cancel any trips.

The grounds around our house are getting fixed and flowers, trees and bushes are being put in. We really had to move fast when the rains started because we're on a hill that had no grass yet. Little by little! Water coming through the faucets is not always there, but we haven't had any major problems since around Easter.

We have electricity more regularly, and one of our neighbors let us hook up to his generators, so if we lose light, we can turn on to his. That's a big relief because of the fridge and the freezer we now have (Patty's!)

How is Joe? Please share my letter with him. Give greetings to everyone—Anne Kelly, Kathleen, Lois S., Alice and Walter, etc, etc—whomever you see!

It's my intention to send a birthday card to David, but I've been interrupted four times already! If I don't make it, please carry birthday greetings to all the July babies!

I'm reading A Distant Mirror currently, a book about the 14th c, which seem to "mirror" many of the happenings of the 19th c. Really interesting. I'm way behind in my reading, generally. Now that the house is arranged, I hope I'll have a little time for myself!

Take care and thanks again for all the thoughtful gifts! Have a good summer and blessings on your works—whatever, wherever!

With love and prayers,
Florence

Letter Thirty-one

30 August 1993

Dear Lois, Carolyn, and Joe,

Hi! How is everyone? I hope the summer was a pleasant one.

Now that a full year has passed, I've managed to write my 1st general letter! I hope you won't mind passing it on for me. We seemed to have lived in the fast lane the whole year. Maybe now that many things are in place, year two will be more relaxed.

I've enclosed the little newsletter Sharon did. I think you might enjoy it. Her little computer makes everything look so professional and nice. She is going to try to do some vocational materials on it for us.

Please greet everyone for me. Carolyn, give special greetings to the scripture group and extend my thanks for the continued subscription to the Christian Monitor!

I hope everyone is well!

With love and prayers,
Florence

Letter Thirty-two

19 April 1994

Dear Lois, Carolyn and Joe,

Hi! Greetings to each of you and to all those I know! I hope you all have recovered from your surgery by now and can enjoy more clement weather! Was the surgery successful?

S. Joan Maier is here, so I've been busy with non-school things. Now I'm writing in haste to dash off a few notes! I'll be home, hopefully, on 29 May, coming into Dallas at 9:20 pm (KLM via Amsterdam). Maybe you can get together with Ruth, David, to see if anyone can meet me. Be sure to let Joan Maier know, or she will probably come too. Her phone is 377-5418.

I had asked Joan to make an early eye appointment for me to be sure I could get the 2nd cataract removed, which she did – June 1st. Carolyn, if I can see your doctors soon after that, it would probably be good. My retreat is the 1st week of July, I think, from around the 3rd, and CND is having some celebrations June 10,11,12 I'd like to attend. Our class (Angie Flynn's) is 35. I would be curious if my cataracts are at all like yours or Joe's – we're all too young to have them. If I'm to have surgery, it would have to be by mid-July so there is time to heal. And then there are all the other doctor checks! – thyroid, tropical disease, gyn, dentist...! I'd love to go to Michigan, Lois, but I don't know how I'll manage!

We are opening a new house in Ikot Ekpene in September and one in Mkar in Benue State. I'll be going to Mkar with Peg Malone, who is coming out newly and who will be the principal of our 1st SSND secondary school for girls. My job is to initiate the building of the complex and oversee it, while Peg apprentices herself to one of the Nigerian principals to learn the Nigerian system of education. Our plan was to be ready for the 1st class in September '95, but who knows?! Things are a bit unpredictable here both politically and economically!

Lois, I saw Elizabeth briefly 2 weeks ago and left the money you sent with Eugenia. The case gets more pathetic each time I see Elizabeth! Without your support group, she would probably be dead by now. However, thanks so much for the financial help, the cards and notes for her. It really means a lot.

Thanks, too, for your letters to me. Carolyn, you are really the expert on the computer – never a mistake! Maybe I'll get some more lessons while I'm recuperating.

We are finally enjoying the new rains! Skies are blue with constant cloud formations, grass is back, flowering tress, and cool breezes! Jos really is a lovely place! Be sure to ask Joan over to share her experiences with you!

I'm so glad Robert is doing well! If it's possible to visit with him and Libby, it would be really nice. I hope you'll help me share this little bit of news and my greetings with whomever you can. Time is running away from me! I want to write Angie and Linda, but I may not make it. Till I can!

Lots of love,
Florence

◀ A March 1st birthday frequently meant a party for Gabe

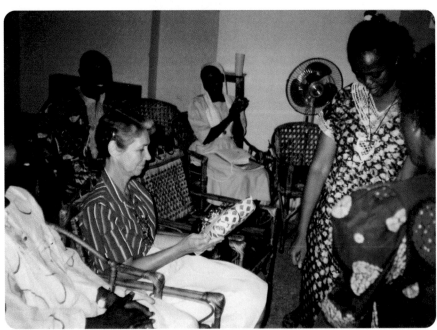

▲ Birthday Celebration

▲ Gabe with Sr. Sharon Dei, 1993

▲ Another birthday party with Sr. Sharon Dei and others
in Jos, March 1, 1994

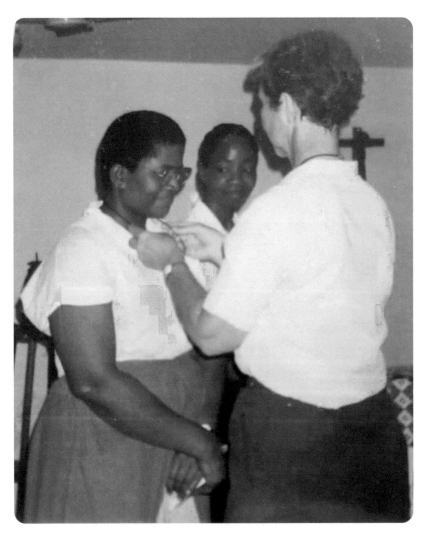

▲ 1994 Sr. Regina Olvah is recieved as a novice by
Sr. Gabriel

1994-1999

Building a School

After a U. S. visit home in the summer of 1994, Gabe returned to a new assignment in Africa. The following years were the most challenging and productive of her time in Africa. A school for girls and a convent were to be built in Mkar, in south central Nigeria. Navigating the formidable bureaucracy of the local government, consulting architects, managing workers, and learning about building materials were all part of her job description. Making the school self-sustaining was a goal, bringing with it the challenge of learning about horticulture and pig raising. Today, the school, Notre Dame Secondary School, thrives and has been ranked among the finest schools in Nigeria.

While in Mkar, Gabe saw that many of the girls' parents and other local residents had never been able to attend school. Responding to that need, she established an adult learning center, dubbed by residents "Sister Gabriel's Evening School." This alertness to the needs of those around her and her generous response to those needs, led the people of Mkar to bestow on her the title "Mure U Tiv" or "Shade of the Tiv."

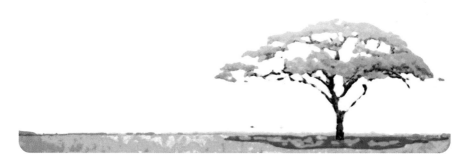

Letter Thirty-three

Roeder Family
August 31, 1994

Thought I would send the fax to you as is.

As usual, Gabriel sounds excited and "in charge." God has gifted her in so many ways. S. Joan

To: Sister Joan Maier
6401 North Charles Street Baltimore, Mb 21212

Fax Number – 410-377•536r3

From: Srs. Gabriel Roeder, Peg Malone,
P. O. Box 2274 Jos, Plateau State. Nigeria
Date: 30 August 1994

Dear Joan,

Hi! We have arrived, safe, sound and a bit travel-weary. Sharon was at Kano with John and the station wagon to meet us, thank God. We were able to get to the 5t.. Louis Convent in – good time well before dark, that is. The one Sister at home there took very fine care of us. We saw two of the newly ordained priests (St Augustine students) there and also delivered Prof. Robinson's letter to his son Dapo.

We drove down to Jos on Monday morning, so Peg got a large dose of new experiences. Dodging pot-holes for 2 hours, looking for petrol, placating the army officers on the road. etc., etc. She saw the varied terrain, the little towns along the way, the rainy-season – sky, the Hausa dress, the rocks of Jos. When we reached the SSND Convent we were welcomed royally. We chatted, unpacked. chatted, went to Mass, prayed. ate and chatted some more.

On Tuesday, today. Gabriel "checked in" at Alien Registration and delivered the various things that were carried for other people. Later in the day we hope to see Archbishop Ganaka to introduce Peg and ask for official "leave" from the Archdiocese for Gabe. If all goes well, we may head for Makurdi on Thursday. Till we see!

Life is very dry here. Petrol is a terrible problem, as usual. so many are walking or biking to get where they want to go. Cooking gas and kerosene are likewise expensive and hard to get. Universities are on strike. However, beyond that, there is no trouble for us. Sharon, Ngozi and Anne are fine and also send their greetings to everyone.

We hope you will relay the word to our families that we have arrived without incident and are being properly welcomed at every turn. It is our intention to fax this tomorrow, Wednesday, and also put a few letters in the mailbag at Hillcrest, just in case. The regular mail is still not working, so hold whatever comes for Sharon in December, unless someone else comes.

Anne is very grateful for your card, your prayers and everything! She is fine now and enjoying her holidays, though she has some extra music lessons with the boys in the parish.

We hear that Bern had a raffia wall put up around the back of the compound in Ikot Etuk Udo and that it is very fine. I don't know if it is considered permanent, but it can be renewed-when needed for the meantime. I will try to find out more.

Sharon has two pieces of vocation literature almost ready for printing! One is on discernment in general, and one on SSND. She has also been working overtime on the committee planning the "canonical election" of the diocese to an archdiocese. Because NEPA has been irregular, she sometimes has to do her typing between 2 and 4 a.m.!

Ngozi said she still has no form! She has her TOEFL – and her SATs. It seems SOME universities are on strike; and in other cases, some DEPARTMENTS are on strike! Distressing, no?

Please give our greetings to Sisters, family and friends! It will be awhile before we get any letters over there.

Lots of love!

Letter Thirty-four

P.O. Box 501 Gboko, Benue State
20 September 1994

Dear Family and Friends,

Msu! My greetings to each of you, – from a different town in a different State, a different language, a different tribe! I pray you are well and finding joy in life.

Peg and I arrived in Kano on schedule and were met by Sr. Sharon and our driver John. What a blessed relief to see them! We went with all our loads to the St. Louis convent in Kano to spend the night, and then set out the next day for Jos. Petrol was still a problem, so we had to watch for black market petrol along the road. Dealing with black market is a new experience for Peg!

We were royally welcomed in Jos, where we only spent a few days. I had to check in at Alien Registration Office and then request a formal transfer at Immigration Office from Jos Diocese to Makurdi Diocese. There were also things to deliver to people that we had carried. It was good to see friends again. The seminarians who had been ordained during the summer were a special pleasure to meet because they were so elated over their ordination!

Although we had tried to contact Bishop Usuh in Makurdi that we had arrived, we had not been able to get through. Peg and I arrived in Makurdi and stayed a night at the Bishop's House. We received the message that we should proceed to Gboko, to St. John's parish. The parish priest (pastor), Fr. Simon Ivever, whom we had been able contact by phone from the Bishop's House, had tracked down the Bishop for us.

When we arrived at St. John's, we were given a small two-room apartment with a bathroom and a large walk in closet. And we have been here since then. Our boxes and suitcases are everywhere! Getting organized seemed impossible at the beginning, but gradually we are finding our way! Luckily, Sr. Sharon and our friend Albert Gonet were able to get a second-hand Peugeot pickup truck for us, so we can move about a bit independently.

There were ever so many small things to do. We had to register with Immigration and Alien Registration in Makurdi, open some additional bank accounts, register the pickup, get insurance, fix a few things on it, etc., etc. These are still not completely finished, but the greater portion has been accomplished.

Peg is in school this morning, trying to learn the Nigerian ropes for administering a secondary school. I'm at home to type some letters to keep the building process going. The geophysical survey to determine the water sites is going to be done this week. The brush has been cut along the boundary of the building site and reinforced cement posts have been ordered which will be placed at the corners and every forty feet to mark the property. Later, it will be completed as a proper fence. We are getting estimates for clearing the site and roads, and also for the building of one staff house which Peg and I will move into. It is also scheduled to sit down with the architect to discuss what is needed so the electrical and plumbing plans can be completed. All of this is part of Phase I. If all goes well, Phase II, which will be the building of the classroom blocks and administration area, will begin in early 1995. However, there is much to be done between now and then!

We have had some very heavy rains lately, though some areas complain of not enough. A dam up in Maidugari broke and destroyed many homes. In another month, we'll be crying for the rain! Petrol is still a problem to find most days, so travel is restricted or expensive. Inflation continues to escalate, the political situation remains a battle of wills. Secondary schools are starting up slowly, but the economy makes paying school fees very hard! Gboko is an important town, the center of Tiv land, but the roads around are mostly in poor condition, making a costly headache for traders and farmers alike. But we are alive and well, and we thank God for life and for one another!

Lots of love,
Gabe

Letter Thirty-five

25 September 1994

Dear Lois and Carolyn,

Hi! Greetings from Gboko! I hope all is well with you there. Things are going fine here, though it seems very slow for both Peg and me. You can't make a flower grow, so we take each day as it comes.

Hopefully, I will enclose a "general" letter with this note. I'd be very glad if you could relay it to others as you have before. Hope you still have the list!

I want to use this note to say a special THANK YOU for all of your generous and thoughtful favors while I was at home. I'm very grateful for the warm and wonderful hospitality, the use of the car, the dinner parties, the extra running and shopping for my sake, the use of the phone, the gifts to bring back-and especially for each of you. Your care and concern were always so evident! And your interest and support of what I'm doing here is a great encouragement. Words are hard to come by to say an appropriate THANKS, but I know you know I am very grateful! Please extend my thanks to Joe has well, and to Ann Kelly, Uncle Ormy et. al, etc., etc.

Today is Sunday, so we are taking it easy. We haven't received any mail, so we are holding our own letters until Sharon comes down for the Area Meeting – we'll give them to her to post via Hillcrest. I'm still checking out the channels of communication. The phone here in Gboko is usually good, but for more than a week it hasn't worked. I'll keep trying!

Take care! Say 'Hi!' to Bill.

Lots of love,
Florence

Letter Thirty-six

March '95

Dear Lois, Carolyn and Joe,

Hi! I hope each of you is fine! Sorry my letter is so late coming – mea culpa! Lois, I hope you will relay it to others as you used to do for me?!

Thanks so much for the letters and all the thoughtful Christmas gifts! They were all just perfect. How I wish I had a tape player in the pickup – I spend so many hours there! I really do appreciate the careful selection of things I like!

Lois, have you retired? Are you still thinking of coming over? The country is not in great shape, as I'm sure you know from the news, but you would certainly be welcome. Give any messages to Joan – I try to call her periodically.

Please give special greetings to Lois Schiaffino for me – and Kathryn, Mimi and Ginny!

I've sent a separate copy of the letter to Dick and Pat Roeder.

Lost of love,
Florence

P.S. Elizabeth is not so fine.

Thanks so much for including my Nigerian friends in the family get-together – was it Thanksgiving? or Christmas?!

Special love to Ann Kelly!

Letter Thirty-seven

March, 1995

Dear Family and Friends,

Msugh! Greetings from Gboko, the heart of Tiv land! After such a long time since hearing from me, you are probably wondering what is happening over here. Well, I am alive and well – and still in Phase I of the building program. I hope everyone there is well and happy and enjoying the signs of Spring. My greetings and best wishes for all the birthdays I've missed, as well!

The Harmattan has gone with its cold and dust. We are in the dry season, praying for the rains to come. The sun is scorching in the afternoons, and the humidity is rising. It's hardly conducive for work, but life goes on. This is the season for meningitis, and it has been very bad this year. People are rushing for the vaccine (which I had before I came!). Some will exploit the situation by increasing the price or by giving only sterile water. There seems to be no control of such things here.

The architect, the painter and the carpenter all had deaths in their immediate families and so had to be away from work. The contractor's driver of his truck has a bad boil and the contractor couldn't find a driver who could manage the gears properly, so he managed with our pick-up. All of this is slowing down the work a bit. Because we haven't yet bought our generator, our borehole is not functioning, so the contractor buys water. If NEPA (electricity) is not working, the water can't be pumped into the water tanker, and that slows up work. Because we have no phones, what you would do by phone, we do by car, and petrol is still a problem here, sometimes very expensive, sometimes scarce. And if NEPA is off, the gas pumps can't work. So doing the simplest things take a much greater investment of time, money and energy here than they would there. Roads and. weather are very, very hard on cars, and inflation refuses to go away. So if we are slow, please understand!!

The goals of Phase I are being accomplished little by little. The boundary was surveyed and some reinforced concrete posts were put up at 40 foot intervals around the site. This, of course, immediately brought protests from some of the land owners whose property touches ours. The procedure for resolving these disputes is a commonplace one, but time consuming. The Chief of Mkar came earlier this week, amid much pomp and circumstance, to walk round the site. He was followed by native drummers (middle-age and older men, in special dress) and lots of school children and other onlookers. He himself was in FINE native attire. This visit signals the near conclusion of agreement, so we are expecting the final document for the land soon. We have ordered some local burnt bricks to build part of the wall which will go round the site. The bricks are large, almost as big as cinderblock, and cost N1.50

to N2.00 – unbelievable in today's market! That is like a dollar and a half or two dollars. The bricks are made by scraping the clay from the bottom of the river Benue, molding them, piling them up in a tent like fashion, and putting a wood fire under them for 4 or 5 days. Firewood has become very costly, so our price will probably be more than we bargained for, but it's the cheapest fence that will still be secure. There will be panels of the brick in between the cement posts, with a few inches in between, so you will be able to see through, but not pass through instead of barbed wire or broken glass being put on the top to keep out thieves (a BIG problem these days) we will plant bougainvillea along the inside, hang over top to the outside. Bougainvillea has huge thorns. Since the clay can be gotten from the river only in the dry season, we will have to wait until next dry season to complete the major portion of the fence.

Another goal of Phase I is the building of a duplex staff house, which will serve as our convent for awhile. This is nearing completion, and is a very strong, attractive, well built house. I keep saying it has to be relatively maintenance free and last until the kingdom comes. We've tried to think of every practical thing we need to be aware of. Whatever has a long life we invest in; if it is easily breakable, we skip it. We have saved lots of money by having a tile roof instead of an aluminum roof, the more common choice for long life. Like myself, most people probably think the tile must be more costly because it is more attractive, but that is not the case. We saved N74,000.00 on this one building.

We also had a geological survey done and a borehole dug. We reached water—abundant and good, deep in the rock under us. It remains for us to "develop" and connect it to the house. An overhead tank is being built, a generator house is being built, and we are in search of a generator that we can afford that will serve our purposes.

Beyond the goals of Phase I, we are bringing NEPA to the site. As it happens, DFRRI (Development of Food, Roads, and

Rural Infrastructure) is now bringing light to the parts of Mkar that are off the main road. The Church made arrangements to have the wire brought up the hill as far as the Church building, so we are continuing it up farther to the site. If the transformer that was installed in the town is commissioned soon, we will be able to enjoy the "light" – everything electric! – as well. If not, we will have our own generator soon.

Other than my work as building director, there are a few other pastimes. One is that I am trying to get the Sisters' Area Conference of Makurdi Diocese reactivated. For about 2 years they have not been meeting. After some preliminary work, I wrote to invite all the convents to a "Gathering" on February 4th. Twenty-eight Sisters responded and three convents sent apologies. All were eager to get back together as a Conference, thank God. We elected temporary officers, who in turn planned a Day of Recollection and Meeting for April 1st. The involvement has been a means of getting to know some of the Sisters better, so I have enjoyed it.

All the Sisters' Conferences of the northern dioceses had a Provincial Meeting in Ilorin, a day's journey from here. The journey was exhausting, the roads wretched, but it was my first time to Ilorin. I met some of my former students from the major seminary in Jos there as newly ordained priests, an added pleasure. The Sisters of Ilorin Diocese had planned many things for us, so the time we spent there was well spent.

I also visit the women in the prison about once a month. The prison is just down the street from where I am living. There are usually about 6 or 8 women, some looking older than I. One of the women delivered a baby while there, and on the next day its eyes swelled and closed with some kind of infection. As usual, there was no money to do anything to help, so I asked if I could help. It meant driving her with 2 guards in the pickup to the hospital. When the doctor said she should be admitted so the baby could get injections, we had to go back to the jail to get 2 different guards to stay with the woman. Luckily, the woman was only there 2 nights. Everyone was so grateful for what I had done for the child, that I think I could ask for the moon and get it now. So I asked for the women to be allowed to join the men on Sundays for Mass. (Prison officials prefer that men and women be separate always. This prevents a priest from going into the women's section.) My request was granted very readily, so last week I attended Mass in the prison with the prisoners. Since I don't really have time to go very often, AND I don't speak Tiv, I was fortunate in getting one of the Nativity Sisters here at St. John's interested in going to the prison also. She goes faithfully every Sunday evening to talk to them and instructs them on the readings of the day. The priest here at St. John's who is in charge of the catechumenate has also promised to include those who are interested in his program, and the president of the Catholic Women wants to go to see what the C.W.O. can do.

Another area of interest is the Remand Home (where juvenile delinquents are "remanded" by the courts). It took about 3 months just to find the place because there is very little interest in it generally. Although the building is relatively new, it was not used for over ten years, so it is infested with bats. Their urine has stained the ceilings and spoiled parts; there is almost NO furniture, and NEPA doesn't work. There is a borehole which can't be used because of no NEPA, and a well which is just about dry now that we are at the end of the dry season. I've been to visit, several times, usually taking someone with me each time who might be able to give some help – priests, sisters, our contractor, etc. I went to a Rotary Club meeting and asked them to visit. Not being able to speak Tiv really limits what I can do myself, though most of the boys "hear" English. Only some speak it. The needs are more than my hand can reach, so getting others interested seems to be the best thing for me to do at present.

There is a woman in the leprosy settlement that I visit about once a month. She depends a lot on charity, so I try to takes something along when I go, but again, I do better if there is a translator present! There is a motherless babies home which I visited only once. The children there are all quite young – under 3, I would say.

Benue Cement Company has something comparable to a "country club" here, with tennis courts, swimming pool, etc. I finally got Fr. Kenny to take me over and introduce me so I could ask for a membership form. As soon as it is I shall be escaping from the hot sun in the pool.

Peg, my partner here, is down in Akwa Ibom until Easter. It was her hope to teach 1 semester, but she has done very little because of the strike. Even when some of the children came back, they were sent home for school fees! Please pray that we will be able to keep our school a private school! Except for private schools, it will be hard to salvage the educational system here. The problems of inflation, corruption, poverty, and discouragement are hard to fight. I saw Peg two weekends ago when I went down to get a carpenter to do our furniture. Because there are far fewer trees up here in the north, carpenters are fewer and far less skilled. Often the wood is not properly seasoned or already full of termites when you buy it up here.

I am staying in our little apartment here in the priest's house at St. John's in Gboko. (Shades of Zaria!) There are 5 priests living here, with whom I eat each day. There is a phone here, which works only infrequently. I was able to get phone calls from my family on Christmas Day, which was a special treat! The second hand pickup we bought we keep in good condition, so we have means to get where we want to go.

Hopefully, this paints at least a vague picture of what I am up to for you! I am in a very safe environment and very well cared for. We have light and water most of the time. There is television in the house with a video, and there is a satellite dish which enables us to get CNN (only). Truthfully, I don't watch it too much, especially now that Peg is not here. I go to the site every morning and every afternoon if I can. Things like laundry (by hand), ironing, mending, cleaning quickly fill in any free time I have, so I don't write many letters unless I am pushed by some deadline or an urgent need. I drive to Otukpo (about an how and a half, partly bad road) now and again to try to call Sister Joan Maier. When I'm successful, the connection is grand!

I wish I could put some of the Tiv music and dance in this letter, or paint some of the lovely scenery for you. Our site is so lovely! A beautiful hilltop. This Nigeria is one vast country, with a great variety of peoples, vegetation, scenery, and climate!

Please excuse me for not writing sooner or more often. Because we are getting very little mail, and that late, it is discouraging. That is no excuse really, but I DO think of you and pray for you often. Each of you is a part of me and whatever I do. So thank for remembering me, for your letters, your Christmas gifts, etc., etc., etc! S. Joan Maier is coming over in mid May for about a month, so if you want to send anything, get it to her.

Lots of love,
Gabe

Letter Thirty-eight

Sr. Mary Gabriel
P.O. Box 501
St. John Roman Catholic Church Gboko, Benue State Nigeria,
West Africa March 22, 1995

Dear Florence,

It seems like such a long time since we talked to you at Christmas time and I'm sure you really miss the mail. People have been asking whether we have heard from you and if you were able to get mail yet. Lois spoke to Joan M. this morning who said there was no regular mail but UPS was getting through. Hopefully this is still true and you will get news once again now we know how to send it to you. Hope both you and Peg are well and your work is moving forward without too many delays. Greet Peg for me.

Since Lois has retired, she has been working hard on the SID's journal as well as her other on-going projects. She has also joined Renew (we are in the same group) and has volunteered to help in providing transportation for parishioners who need it. So she is as busy, if not busier, as ever.

I am glad to see the winter season gone. It has been full of flu, colds and other viruses for many. March came in like a lamb with mild temperatures so we are out doors once again with yard cleanup. The snow drops have multiplied and lasted all through February and are just now fading, crocus are bobbing bright yellow and purple, the daffs and forsythia have popped open this week, and there is a tinge of green on shrubs and lawn. We decided to have a friend of Lois' who is a landscape architect come and draw up some plans for some ideas we would like to do, like relaying the brick sidewalk, running drip hoses and a pipe with faucet for easier watering in the garden area and now that the big oak on the side is gone we have an area for a sunny flower bed. Charles even came on a Saturday morning to guide Lois on how to prune shrubs. It is only a beginning but what a difference it makes. I have as usual been ripping the ivy from under the shrubs – so far I've not been in the poison variety.

Dixie will be three years old tomorrow. Her winter coat is heavy and she seems to have more black on her. Lois says the fur between her toes is white. Her ears are still a problem but not as bad as I expected during the cold weather. She would shake her head a lot but at least her ears were not wet and swollen.

Lois and Ruth and Joe are flying about these days. Lois to California for a week of vacation and then the annual Neuro-Chemistry meetings, Ruth to London theaters and Joe to Seattle, Washington for a training and to California to visit a friend and then Ohio in May for three weeks of training. In April, Lois and I will spend a weekend in Virginia at Chincoteague for bike riding.

The group has done as much as we wanted on the Care of the Soul. On the last meeting we saw the video which Erin taped, and discussed it. The tape seemed to help bring Thomas Moore into a more personable being. Some still had difficulty with the book though. Alberta has not been well enough to be with the group throughout the winter and June Lunney will be moving closer to her work at N.I.H. and we will be losing her also. The group is definitely shrinking.

I hope Sharon was able to carry back things for you from us at Christmas. She seemed to be in over-load as you were going back.

Must go now, errands to run. Love,
Carolyn

P.S. We just got your letter on 3/27, and inquired about U.P.S. which would be about $75 to mail a letter!

Letter Thirty-nine

23 April 1995

Dear Ange,

Hi! How are you? I pray all is well. This letter is so old now (March, 1995), and I'm sure you've seen it already. But I remember that you liked to save them, so I wanted to be sure you received your own copy. I save the long letters until last – so here I am 6 weeks later!

I did get a letter from you many moons ago. All sounded well. Thanks so much for keeping in touch. Our life is so irregular, and we're still living out of suitcases, stepping over boxes, mislaying things! We're really looking forward to moving into the staff house (temporary convent) on site.

Phase I is still not finished, but we're getting closer. In the meantime, I've signed the contract for Phase II, classroom and administration blocks, and the contractor has begun clearing the top of the hill. He will be making his own cement blocks this time because the project is bigger than Phase I. It will mean jobs for lots of folks, – praise God!

There is so much "struggle" connected with the most ordinary things in life here! Some days it's hard to get myself above it to see what else is going on. In fact, there is so much good that has grown out of the project, it is very touching. There is a real sense of community among the workers – concern, helpfulness, humor. And the villagers are so happy with the progress. The house we have is well built and attractive, though simple. They (the villagers) are delighted that they have been chosen to have such a place in their midst. One said they feel the whole of Mkar is beautiful now because of our building. God has been very good to us – a gorgeous site, an outstanding architect, and excellent contractor, scores of friends, supporters and well wishers.

The financial aspect is the most stressful but maybe God wants to make the point that, in the end, it is God who builds and prospers, not us, not even the mighty American dollar – which seems to be controlling the whole world!

Dear Ange, I think of you so often! Sometimes I feel like you're here. It would be great to just pick up a phone and call, wouldn't it? I miss you, Ange! And I praise God for the beautiful strong woman you are!

With lots of love,
Gabe

Letter Forty

Summer, 1995

Dear Lois, Carolyn and Joe,

Hi! Greetings from Notre Dame, Mkar! We have packed into our new house, finally – 3 of us: Peg and I and a novice, Chiniyere. I hope Joan Maier will share pictures and stories with you.

Thanks so much for the gifts – I think the video and book are from you. Some of your Christmas gifts are beautifying our house – crucifix and picture of Madonna of the Way. And thanks too for your letters and fax. I did get them all. I have to pay $80.00 a page for fax, but at least now I know to ASK if there is anything for me when I go to Nital! (Which is not all that often!) I hope you are all well and enjoying life.

Lois, it sounds like you are settling into a new rhythm that you can enjoy!

Life has been extra busy and hectic these last several weeks, but we try to keep sane!

Please give love to everyone for me!

Lots of love to you,
Florence

Letter Forty-one

Summer, 1995

Dear Lois,

Hi! Greetings to you and all the family! Hope you have received my general letter via Sharon.

I've heard from Patty Wood Wilson – she is in Jos, just about 3 hrs. away. I hope to visit soon.

Elizabeth Sampson fell and broke her wrists last year. She was slow in getting medical attention, so they didn't heal well. That's probably partly why her writing has become so poor. A pitiful creature! I gave the money to Fidelis Akpan. He and Dr. Udoakang are checking out an offer of land in her village if she builds a house. Do pray for her. Any little note will encourage her.

The new house is quite pleasant, but still with wrinkles to be ironed out. The stove doesn't work, toilet doesn't flush, no light in my bedroom or the bathroom... But it is nice! Little but little!

I hope your birthday is very special!

With lots of love,
Florence

Letter Forty-two

Fall, 1995

Dear Lois, Carolyn and Joe,

Hi! I hope all is well! Sorry I'm so poor in writing-maybe our bulletin will substitute! I've enclosed extras for whatever folks might be interested—Ann K., Alice, etc.

I'll send a bunch to Angie for the scripture group, Carolyn.

The mango season has come and gone; now we are into oranges and ground nuts. Mkar is great for this alone!

Please greet all!

Lots of love,
Florence

Letter Forty-three

W/ Africa
3 December 1995

Dear Lois,

Greetings from Nigeria the giant of Africa! I hope it's all fine with you and your family. I am fine here in school and preparing for the end of the semester's exams.

I wish to write and thank you a million times for your charity and generosity – the expensive, precious and beautiful gift you send to me through your Sister, Sr. Gabriel Roeder SSND. This gift is so beautiful and expensive that I cannot afford to buy one even after my seminary training. I have given it (the piano) a name "KASHAMM" meaning beautiful in my tribe – BAJJU, Kachina State, Nigeria. In fact, I lack adequate words to express my profound gratitude to you. I simply pray that God may also show you his mercy, charity, and love; may He continue to strengthen you in good health of mind and body. May God also bless all your family in the same way.

May you please remember me in your family daily prayers as I always have you in my daily prayers because I still have a long way to go on my journey to the priesthood. I still have three and a half years to go.

Thanks once more, and may God bless. I shall be waiting to hearing from you.

With love and prayerful wishes,
Abraham Adamu Kunat

Letter Forty-four

School Sisters of Notre Dame
Nigeria
10 January 1996

Dear Family, Friends and Strangers,

Msugh ne! My greetings to everyone – Merry Christmas, Happy New Year, Happy Birthday, Happy Anniversary, Happy Thanksgiving – everything since I've last written. I am alive and well mid still living in Mkar (pronounced "Mkah" in Nigerian English!) You may think I'm a stranger at this point for not writing or maybe just strange. My excuses are the same as always, so please allow me to omit them this time.

Peg Malone, my partner here in Mkar, should be home by now on her leave, to be back by Easter. The 3rd member of our community is Ngozi, who is a student at the Univ. of Nsukka working toward her B.A. So at the moment I am alone. There, are a few young women who are. aspiring to join us who sometimes visit, so I am not always alone.

We are in the dry season here, which sometimes has some cool winds, especially at night. However, it never seems to get really cold. We don't even have blankets in the house. The grasses are tall and very dry everywhere, so the current sport for young boys is to burn the grass so they can catch the field mice – to eat or sell. The ground is very hard from the dryness, but in spite of that and the burning, there is still plenty green around. A day or two after a burning, you can always see some little patch of new green grass in the midst of the ashes! God is wonderful!

Our borehole is still not functioning, so we are buying water. That has hurt us and the construction company, which is making the cement blocks right here on site. We both keep hoping, but it is so hard and so frustrating trying to make things work here. But we keep trying! In spite of that hardship, our little house runs smoothly. We have light from NEPA as well as a generator; we have our trusty little pick-up, and lots mid lots of friends. So we are O.K. here!

The project is moving along well. The roof tiles are going on and that is slow because it has to be done so carefully. They tell me the roof is as important as the foundation. The roof tiles are made here in Benue State. (We have only 3 large industries in Benue, all of which suffer from poor management!) The tiles are a clay color and look very lovely. They are also keeping us cool, thank God! When you are in Gboko and look toward our site (on the back side of Mkar Hill), you can now see a patch of pink in the midst of the. trees. That's the roof of Notre Dame Secondary School! Alleluia!

The carpenters are also busy putting in window and door frames and ceilings. Most workers have not yet come back from their Christmas break. When they do, I think they may start plastering.

Peg and I wrote many grants. So far we have received one from the Dutch Embassy here for the furnishings of the home-ec lab. We also received a large grant for furnishings and equipment from our Sisters in Bavaria and Sweden. There are a few others that we are hopeful of getting, but we've had several refusals. Education is not a high priority in the world right now, even though it is probably one of the most crippling problems in this country at the moment. So we are still struggling for money.

In trying to be cost-efficient, I came across a brick making machine, which uses no energy. France has been the leader in trying to encourage and improve ways of using the earth for building houses. Of course, there are many houses built of mud or clay in Nigeria. Different cultures have different designs. The machine we have makes compressed laterite bricks which are dried naturally. Some small cement is added after the mixture of the laterite has been tested. Originally, I thought only of completing our fence with the bricks. After some investigation, I found you can build anything you would with clay bricks at home, so I got very excited! We have begun making sample bricks and testing them for strength (after sending 2 men to Jos for training!). If the wall is a success, we will try to build the cafeteria with them. We want that building to be in the style of the Tiv eating places. It looks like a very large gazebo with a straw roof a type of grass the lasts quite long and is very slow to burn. It is protected from sun and rain, but catches the breezes. Natural air conditioning! I would love to be able to show the people in the area how such an environmentally-friendly procedure can work successfully!

Elijah, our supervisor for the project, is also supervising the brick making. We hired a new man, Yarkwan, who is a deaf mute. We knew him from St. John's in Gboko where he used to wash the Fathers' clothes. He is probably not more than 30 and is married to a young woman whom he met in the School for the Deaf; she is also deaf and mute. They now have a little girl who seems to have good hearing. Yarkwan is bright and hard working. He had been after us for long to find work for him here, so when this opportunity presented itself, he came to mind right away. His presence has opened up a whole new dimension of communication for everyone here. Elijah is the best in communicating with him, but we all try! Yarkwan is really happy to be here and to be able to work just one job that enables him to support himself and his family. (He had 3 before.) Hopefully, families who have a deaf child at home will see Yarkwan and send the child to school!

Our visits to the boys in the Remand Home, the women in prison, the orphans, and the folks in the leprosy settlement continue to teach us many things. Perhaps the thing we've done for them that has helped the most is to make others more aware of them. Most people don't even know where the places are! But they are always so happy when they have visited; it is a touching experience every time.

Many hours are spent in the pick-up, going to Makurdi, up to Jos or down to Akwa Ibom, doing what might be done by phone or mail if such things were in place and worked. Many hours are spent "waiting for Godot" – at the bank, the Water Board, or here, waiting for the architect or the lawyer, who never come! It feels like running in place – getting nowhere fast. However, it is the only way available here, so we continue on the road that has brought us thus far!

We are often being pleasantly surprised by the number of young women who come or who write that they are interested in joining SSND. We had a few of them here after Christmas. They joined us in the daily routine and we talked to them about the call to religious life and the need to discern that. We prayed and played and sang and ate together. We helped them write their letters of application and fill the forms. Then we had a Mass here in the house during which we prayed especially for them and gave them each a medal of Mother Theresa Gerhardinger, our foundress. They were so thrilled and happy! And what they loved most was the experience of community! That was a WOW for us, because that is an essential ingredient of our charism! God is really wonderful. And I would say Mother Theresa is working overtime!

Lots of love,
Florence

Letter Forty-five

SSND Generalate
Roma, Italia
8 June 1996

Dear Family and Friends,

My greetings to you all! I pray you are well, have enjoyed birthdays, anniversaries, etc. that have been taking place. As you well know, our mail is terrible, but I do get some news of what is happening when someone travels back or forth. For all the notes, gifts and moral support, my heartfelt thanks!

We have just finished an intense meeting here at the Generalate discussing the possibility of the various African missions becoming a province in the congregation. Everyone agrees we will do that, but we have to wait for some modalities to be worked out. Usually new provinces are formed by breaking them off from large provinces; we are coming at the reality from the other side. We are small mission extensions asking to be a single entity, even though we are not self sufficient. Nevertheless, our leadership is completely behind us and involved in the homework that lies ahead.

It was an exciting international experience here for us, as our Polish sisters are here, one sister from Germany and one from Switzerland, several tribes/countries from Africa and our Americans. These gatherings give a great boost to me because you can see the powerhouse we have in the congregation: faith-filled, dynamic, intelligent women with a wonderful assortment of gifts. It is so great to be a part of them! Sister Kyllene, my 5th grade teacher from St. Mark's was here, just returning home from Kenya.

Some of the Nigerian contingent went back yesterday because of school on Monday, some are staying to make retreat, and the rest of us are going tomorrow. We are all fine, if a bit tired! The hospitality was grand and we were spoiled with any and every goody that isn't found easily in Africa – like ice cream, chocolate, cheese, etc., etc., etc.! We are all a bit heavier as we leave!!

Peg and I got a little shopping in for things like tapes for the typewriters we received from the British Embassy and for our word processor, a good pair of pliers, etc. We also visited St. Peter's briefly and found our way home on the train. We will return to a lot of work at the school, so please keep us in your prayers! The problem of water is still unsolved, after 5 attempts at boreholes. The efforts are eating up the money as well as our time and energy. We have a consultant who has offered some attractive ideas to solve the problem; it remains to see the price tag that will be put on the ideas! We are still busy writing grants for the furnishings of the school and the construction of the convent. Rains have made the work we are doing to control erosion take a high priority. Thank God we had done all that was done! However, there is yet more. The making of our own laterite bricks is moving very successfully, and the bricks go into our fence around the school. Unfortunately, this becomes more and more important as we equip the school with electrical and plumbing appliances, furniture, typewriters, etc. – all of which our thieves love! The laterite road inside the school compound is nearing completion, after much, much difficulty and disagreement with our contractor. The school proper is moving along, slowly but surely. The newest date for handover is the end of June for JSS (Junior Secondary School) and Administration; mid-August for SSS (senior Secondary School).

The Catholic Common Entrance Exam was given, and Peg has selected names for 2 classes of girls for JSS 1. For those in the immediate area who did not pass, a remedial year of study will be offered to precede the regular JSS 1. We are doing all possible to make quality education available to those who never get that opportunity. The school is private, so there will be tuition, but we are providing the desks for students and some of the textbooks, and we will have equipment in the school – which is not true generally in any government school and sometimes not even in private schools. Of course, we hope the commitment of the teachers and their fidelity to their tasks will be an evident difference from what the poor children in government schools have seen! Because the school is well built, strong and beautiful, we are constantly pressured to make it a boarding school so many could come from distances. However, the poor girls could never afford the boarding fees and they would be out-classed by the competition of those who are from wealthy families and who have attended better primary schools. So we are doing a new thing, and it feels like swimming upstream! Do pray we can make this work.

We have received cash donations from our families and friends, from our Sisters in Sweden and Bavaria; we have grants from the Dutch Embassy here for the equipment in the home-ec lab (sewing machines, stoves, fridges); we have a grant from the Canadian Embassy to help is with overhead water tanks and to assist with our predicament of getting an adequate water supply; we have a grant from 3-Kings in Action which will help build the desks and chairs; we have a grant from British Embassy for 20 new manual typewriters for the students and one electric one for the principal's office, plus money for math and English textbooks; we have a promise from Missio to pay for one fourth of the cost of constructing the convent if we are able to get the full amount. Through Bernard Hobbs, the Knights donated Mass vestments for the school. We have been greatly blessed and we are very, very grateful! The work of asking for help continues: we need to equip the science labs in SSS, build more desks and furniture, complete the cost for the building of the convent and furnish the convent – and there are other buildings for the school to be constructed down the road (like a cafeteria, assembly block, library and additional staff houses. We try to take 1 day at a time and do the best we can. If anyone is able to help us, be assured of our prayers for you daily!

Two of our newly professed Nigerians will be coming to Notre Dame, Mkar to be on the staff for September, thanks be to God! Peg has hired her vice-principal of academics – a Tiv priest who has had experience in the arena of education. She has been very busy interviewing the many folks who have come to apply to teach in our school.

Our animals now include 3 ducks, 2 goats, a dog and cat, 3 turkeys, 3 rabbits, and several chickens. We have planted yam, groundnut, corn, guinea corn and cassava, not to mention the trees and flowers that are part of the erosion-prevention scheme. From our groundnut harvest of last year, we were able to make our own groundnut paste (peanut butter) and it was delicious!

I know some of you have been sick or had surgery in recent months, some have lost a loved one, some have retired; some suffered from other problems that caused hearts to be heavy. My own heart is with you in all that life affords. May God's strength and patience be with you!

This is the second time I am typing a letter, as I lost the first one on this computer. Let me try to print it in time to send back to the States with someone here!

With love and prayers,
Florence/Gabriel

Letter Forty-six

Notre Dame, Mkar
Benue State, Nigeria
16 September 1996

Dear Family and Friends,

Greetings to each of you! I pray all is well with you as you leave summer breaks behind and move into a new autumn season. We are in the rainy season still, here. The rains will soon become less and less though; October is usually the last month for rain in this part of the country. I always hate to see the rains go. The skies are especially beautiful after the rains: very blue and very clear. Sometimes we can see the mountains east of us, probably in the Cameroons. Rains do a terrible job on the roads, however!

Notre Dame Secondary School opened on 9 September 1996. It was really exciting for us all. We have to streams of JSS I (Junior Secondary School I Elementary 7) and 1 Remedial Class for those girls in the immediate parish who didn't pass the entrance exam. It will be a pre-JSS I, hopefully. We are trying to be sensitive to the people who gave us the land for the school. All together there will be about 100 girls when everybody is here. S. Peg had classes the first day, even though most schools had neither students nor classes. Cutting the grass is the agenda for most schools, so the kids don't come; and then some don't have their school fees.

Our school compound is still a building site, and we do not have water flowing into the school yet. We did have a well dug and a pump and a tank installed to make temporary provisions. This seems to be working fine, thank God. The big, main tank will be here by 1st October. When it is in place, the water from our redeemed borehole will be pumped into it and from there to the school. As you might guess there are volumes I could write in between the above lines about what has been happening, but I will spare you!

We have $25,000.00 tied up in Lobi Bank that can't be released to us because they are not in the Clearing House. So I spend a lot of time chasing after the money! Lately, it has meant running up and down to Makurdi at least once a week, but I think soon I will have a schedule from them for getting the money back little by little. It may take almost two years! However, I'm grateful the money wasn't lost in the bank crises, and as soon as the return is in place and working, I hope to head for the States. Early October, maybe?

Our little school is a very solid and very lovely building. The name Notre Dame is on everyone's lips. People come from far and wide to see the place. You wouldn't see anything extraordinary in it, but most schools here are built in a haphazard manner without any plan. Buildings are stuck anywhere, and generally are never fully finished. Seldom are they painted. That we planned ours, built the entire block of classrooms, labs and administration, painted it and planted flowers. makes it unique. Even adults are wishing they were young enough to go to school again. And everyday Peg is turning away late comers who want to take the entrance exam! That she kept to a schedule for entrances and that she doesn't show favors is also unique here. However, the word has gone out that if you want to get into Notre Dame, you must study hard because you must pass the entrance exam. We are being warned that next year there will be a mighty flood of applicants! May we live up to the expectations!

Our SSND community here in Mkar is four this year: S. Peg the Principal, S. Bessie, math teacher, S. Regina, Health and Phys. Ed. teacher, and myself, Building Director. We are living in one half of the duplex staff house. Father Didacus Kajo, our Vice Principal and resident chaplain, lives in the other half. Most rooms there are still used for storage, but he has a bedroom and a bath and "manages." He says Mass for us most days in our parlor and he often eats with us.

You may have heard that we were attacked by armed robbers in July. Because of that we now have an armed policeman on duty each night. We keep working on the wall around the compound, but the site is big, so it is costly. We are making our own laterite bricks to build the fence and it looks lovely. We are planting bougainvillea bushes, with their mighty thorns, to climb over the wall and make it more lovely.

We have gotten gifts and grants to help us with the school. The British High Commission gave us typewriters and textbooks, Canada helped us with the water problem, the Dutch Embassy gave us sewing machines, stoves, fridges and cookers for the home-ec lab. Other monetary gifts enabled us to buy desks and chairs and build the tables in the science lab. There is loads more to do to furnish the JSS, but we certainly have enough to start and start well. We have lots more than most schools. We would like people to see what schools would be like if money went where it was supposed to! The furnishing of the Administration and the SSS (Senior Secondary) still remain in front of us. Someone from the Japanese Embassy is visiting us on the 25th of this month and we will be asking for a school bus. If they cannot manage that one, we will ask them to help us furnish the Biology lab for SSS. There are some other requests out there that we are still waiting to hear about.

We would love to start the convent soon, as we are already crowded in the 3-bedroom Staff house. We have some of the funding promised, but not all, so we are still working toward that. I would also like to get at least the dining part of the cafeteria built (with our laterite bricks) to serve as an assembly hall for the school for the meantime.

We had a wonderful Assembly of the Whole (of Africa) in Rome in early August. Africa will soon become a District of the Congregation, a first step to becoming a province. There has been lots on the agenda in that area! We have lots happening, too, with young women asking to enter. There is much work in getting to know them and helping the get prepared to enter. This January we have 8 fine young women entering, all educated beyond secondary school.

I am alive and well! I think of you often!

Lots of love,
Gabriel (Florence)

Letter Forty-seven

Notre Dame, Mkar
P.O. Box 501 Gboko
Benue State
18 November 1996

Dear Family and Friends,

Merry Christmas and Happy New Year to all! and accumulated best wishes for Happy Birthdays and Anniversaries, Valentine's Day, Easter, etc., etc., etc. I hope you are all-well and happy. I'm really sorry I have been such a poor writer. My thanks to those of you who wrote anyway! I do love to hear news from home.

We are in the heat and harshness of the harmattan. The world is dry and getting a bit colorless. Everything is dusty, the sky is grey – a winter in the language of the tropics, I guess. It is the season of bees and bushfires (deliberate – to flush out the rats for eating), scorpions and snakes.

Change of seasons is always a time of added sickness here. This time it is respiratory-related mostly, though other standbys are ever present, especially malaria and typhoid. Thanks be to God we are all fine. The dust gives me the sneezes, and I had one cold.

When I look in the mirror I marvel at how old I am looking, and I certainly don't have the energy I used to, but since I'm – almost 60, that is probably O.K.

Peg and I get to the swimming pool now and. again, just to get away from all the busyness here. We try to socialize and now and again we host some friends for dinner. And then there is Sister Bessie who loves to play games after supper! She forces me to relax instead of going back to the typing.

Our little school, Notre Dame Mkar is in session and doing fine. We have two classes of JSS I, each with about 35 students; then we have a remedial class of about 27. The latter, are getting a strong dose of math and English in the hope that they will be able to pass the entrance exam to JSS I next year. They are all from our immediate parish. Only one child from the-parish passed the exam and is in JSS I – and she was raised and schooled in Kaduna! That should give you an idea of the academic standards here. Except for some of the private schools, the children who leave primary school, especially those in the "bush," are left bankrupt. They can't read, write, they can't speak or hear English. That means they can't enter secondary school, so their future is bleak for them. We are trying to redeem the situation and salvage those who have the academic ability to go further.

We have one girl who is the first girl from her village ever to attend secondary school; we have one who is paying her own way by raising groundnuts and selling them, all on her own. Many of our girls walk to school from Gboko everyday – an hour walk I would guess. Going home in the afternoon tropical sun is no fun thing! If I happen to pass any students in the pickup, I fill up fast!

The girls look fine in their blue uniforms, (patterned on that of Notre Dame Prep), and they seem very happy and excited to be here. Sister Peg and the staff are working hard and beginning to see encouraging results. We are offering them quality education where teachers teach every day. We have equipment in the labs and for phys ed – simple and minimal by U.S. standards, but a luxury for them. We have our benefactors to thank for that! We had student desks and chairs made for the students and bought textbooks for them to use – two uncommon things for here.

So there is progress; it is just that it is always much slower than we expect it to be. We are making progress with the water situation and the erosion problems, but that is also very slow and very expensive. I spend a good third of my life writing grants and trying to follow them up. I feel like a professional beggar most days! We are trying to get a school bus from the Japanese Embassy right now, plus some help with furnishing and equipping the science labs in the SSS. Pray for us! The men from the Embassy were so interested in us, because one of them knew the SSNDs in Japan and the great work they are doing there. We are really very hopeful.

We still have 2 million naira ($25,000.00) tied up in Lobi Bank. I could write a book about that topic!! The running up and down, back and forth! I can only keep chasing them for the money, but it is exhausting, back and forth to Makurdi. If I don't get the money we cannot pay the contractor. The grace of the moment is that the contractor is having his own cash problems because the government has not paid for his work for them! So he has slowed down his work here; he can't ask for any payments. My pain is that I must still pay salaries to the architect, the supervisor and the quantity surveyor, and that hurts. However, God manages to keep us afloat.

Life is full of humor, intended and not intended, frustrations and painful sadness, wonderful people and little miracles every day. Because of the construction, there is constant activity that butts into our house. We have a full time water ministry – going to the fridge to get cold water for the workers. Interruption is our second apostolate! But we keep on trying.

We are active in the Sisters Area Conference, Peace and Justice issues, and we do a good amount of work with the poor who can't get help or attention easily, like the lepers, the kids in the Remand Home, women prisoners, etc., but actually, the poor are around us always and begging for something from us always – work, an advance in pay, the use of the pickup to carry their soybean or dead grandmother, etc., etc., etc. There is no time to get into trouble, I assure you.

If anyone among you is a good fund raiser, we need all the help we can get to keep things moving here: Even a little goes a long way! If you can line some churches or other organizations up for me, I'll visit them when I come home.

I do hope you will relay my greetings to everyone. I don't know when I will be coming home yet; maybe next summer? I hope we will still recognize one another! Do take care of yourselves for me!

With lots of love,
Florence/S. Gabe

Letter Forty-eight

Sunyani, Ghana
24 August 1997

Dear Family and Friends,

My greetings to each of you from Sunyani! I pray all is well there and you are enjoying the end of summer activities. I want to send at least a few words along with one of the Sisters who is traveling to the States in a few days, though I don't have lots of news.

When Peg, Sharon and I arrived in Ghana, we stayed one day in Nsawam with our Sisters before getting a small plane

(2 propellers) as far as Kumasi. The flight was 30 minutes and saved us 4 or 5 hours' drive over poor road. Deo gratias!! Sr. Mary Ann, who was driving to the same meeting from Cape Coast, met us there. We had lunch – a hamburger no less! – and drove the rest of the journey to Sunyani (an hour and a half). Sharon had to come from Nigeria by road, so we were glad this piece of the journey was shortened.

The meeting went well. It was good to see and be with old friends, and our agenda was certainly challenging. This new African District has to organize itself in many ways and communications across country boundaries are difficult – Nigeria especially. Because of my jet lag, I found the inactivity of sitting for long periods of time for several days very tiring. Others were tired for different reasons, but we managed to complete the agenda. One of the items we had to grapple with was whether or not we should send our Sisters back to Sierra Leone yet. Their Bishop had asked them to return. The events of the last few days have certainly put that off for awhile! We were fortunate to have Sr. Dorez as facilitator and Srs. Peg and Eleanor as secretaries, so we left with minutes in hand and lots of homework. The next Leadership Meeting will be in Nigeria in November! Sharon left mid-meeting after she and Delmarie (who was a tremendous help to the Sisters with computer lessons while she "hung around") gave their input and gathered information for the communications grant for Shalom. Peg began her retreat when the meeting was finished. The Ghana Area is having their Area Meeting now and celebrating birthdays and jubilees and departures. I'm happy to be able to sit in on it, because I am interested to hear the reactions of the Sisters to the reports coming from Leadership Meeting we just had and compare their meeting process with our own in Nigeria. There are 18 Sisters here, including one from Germany, one from Canada and one from Switzerland. There is only one indigenous Sister. The population is quite different from our own in Nigeria. Where we have 9 indigenous sisters and 8 Americans, one of whom is

Canadian. The meeting closes tonight. Tomorrow morning, I will drive to cape Coast with Mary Ann and help her move into their new house. I can only stay a few days, but she is glad for extra hands, as everyone else is otherwise occupied at the moment. I will return to Nsawam on Wednesday to meet Peg and prepare for our flight to Nigeria on the 29th. Exactly what I will do when I reach there depends on whether planes are available and which places they are flying to. We live one day at a time and catch the surprises as they fall!

Sr. Marie Antoinette drove Sr. Sylvia to the airport after the Leadership Meeting, so she was down in Nsawam when the news came that Sr. Cecilia's mother died. Celie was en route up here by car at the time! So Marie Antoinette stayed down a couple of extra days to help get Celie on a plane home. The discernment for the new Novice Director is the next big item on her agenda. That will be in Kumasi at the Pastoral Centre the 27th to the 29th. It's a pity Peg and I will not be able to hear the results before we leave Ghana, but maybe we can call from Lagos.

I was very blessed at British Airways coming over with my many pieces of luggage. They charged me nothing extra for additional pieces or for overweight. However, I am not sure I will move so easily for the rest of my journey. Since I am with Peg, I will take it all as far as Lagos anyway. Then it depends on the "surprises."

We are still in the raining season here, so we have had many overcast days, showers at night, and showers all day yesterday. It is damp sometimes, humid sometimes. Generally, however, the rains have not been much. It is hard to get the laundry dried some days, but there has been some sun, for a bit at least, on most days. This area of Sunyani is apparently very good for roses. They grow well and with little trouble.

Our novices, Irene and Nentaweh, are fine. They are preparing for their first profession on 4th October. I will be returning to Ghana for that, and they have asked me to give the homily. There is a new community forming here in Sunyani because the Formation House needs space for the new postulants coming next month. They call themselves the Sojourners. They have been asked to stay in the Novitiate for the period that it will be empty. A new house for the Sisters is going to be built at Notre Dame Secondary School, and they will move there in the future.

Space tells me I should close. Take care, all!

With love and prayers,
Gabriel

Letter Forty-nine

25 Aug. 1997

Dear Lois and Carolyn,

Hi! I hope all is fine.

Enclosed is a letter for circulation, if you will, please. I'd be grateful if you send one to Joan Maier at the Motherhouse. I have 3 – one for you, one for Ruth and one for Sharon.

Sorry! I came away with your Ace bandage! It came in very handy, as I used it once here.

Thanks so very much for all your love and support, – in every possible way – while I was home. I hope I wasn't a burden. Your interest, help and presence say a great deal and mean a lot to me. May God bless you as generously and graciously as you have blessed me!

Don't forget Patty Wilson on the list of people who get my letter. And add whoever you think appropriate and you can afford! Please say "Hi" to everyone, especially Joe.

With love and prayers,
Florence

Letter Fifty

TO: Sharon Dei SSND
FAX: (412) 920-6791
DATE: 2 Sept. 1997
FROM: M. Gabriel Roeder

Hi, Shar! How are you? And how are you "managing?" I pray Jeannie is doing well. Please give her greetings for me. Tell her I miss our ice cream deserts for supper together!

I am going up to Jos tomorrow and thought I would try to get a fax out to you. Peg and I got home about 6 pm on Saturday. We had arrived Lagos almost midnight on Friday, so we stayed at a "Marriott" Hotel. Saturday was sanitation Saturday, so we gratefully slept in. We did try to call Fr. Dan and Mrs. Robinson, but were unsuccessful.

I need to see Nentaweh's aunt to tell her she is invited by Sr. M. A. to the ceremony on 4th October. I want to share some of the information from the meeting and give the dates of upcoming events to the sisters as well. There is other "homework" for me as well, so I will probably be there a few days.

I have a date with Igba on Sunday, and then I will head for Akwa Ibom to repeat the sharing of information and meet with Carol and the Formation Team if possible. I will also see our new postulants. It's a shame I can't get there before the 8th, but...not possible! From Akwa Ibom I will go to Benin and see Irene's Dad about his invitation, then possibly to Lagos to buy plane tickets or make reservations for the celebration on the 4th. Then home again.

While I was in Ghana I visited Packy. I gave him your address, phone and fax numbers, so I hope he writes. He seems the same, but his hearing is poorer than it was. He complained of pain in his thigh, which slowed him down and held him back a bit, but he is still going great guns! He drove me back to Nsawam, but wouldn't get out of the car. I didn't want to push having him climb all those steps, so I left it. As it turned out, no one was home!

You will be happy to hear the good news that Fr. Moti has just been appointed head of CIWA. Everyone is so happy and excited for him! He goes down on Sunday to be introduced to the school by the new Papal Nuncio and some visitors from Rome. May he do well!

The Synod here in Makurdi was a big success. What I've heard so far has been very positive. There are changes out for the priests, and we are losing John Ikponko. How we will miss him! We heard that Makurdi has received money from Rome for a radio station. Interested? The Bishop is also working toward making St. T. A. a Major Seminary having theology, so he is looking to send priests to study to be prepared for that – and other areas as well, of course.

We didn't get to discuss the Newsletter at our Team meeting, but we did talk about it some outside the meeting and everyone is very positive about having it. No doubt something will be settled at our next meeting – here, in early December. I want to suggest an article for you to work on: we have three former provincials here and at least one former councilor; we had Eunice before. If you could send them some questions to answer, perhaps you could put an interesting article together that would be good PR and propaganda for us!

Gabe

Letter Fifty-one

Notre Dame, Mkar
P.O. box 501
Benue State
29 September, 1997

Dear Family and Friends,

My greetings to each of you from Mkar! I pray every one is well and finding a way to enjoy whatever you are doing! All is well here, thank God!

Time is passing so quickly. I am getting ready to go to Ghana for the First Profession of two of our novices. Since I will see S. Marie Antoinette in Ghana, and she is going to the States on 10 October, I'm trying to take advantage of the connection. Mail, phone and fax are all sluggish here, as many of you already know. I've been trying to track down email connections since they seem to work so much better and are so much cheaper, but that is not so simple. However, I keep trying.

After our Leadership Meeting in Ghana in mid-August, I hung around while Peg made her retreat and enjoyed myself. The SSNDs were having their Area Assembly, so I attended. Then I went down to Cape Coast to help S. Mary Anne move into the new convent, but it wasn't quite ready, so three of us toured a bit. We went to the museum at Cape Coast, one of the big slave deporting stations in days past, to Kakum Rain Forest, and we walked the beach. Mary Anne took us out to eat a couple of times right on the ocean, which was lovely. So I relaxed. On my way back to Nsawam to meet Peg, I stopped in Accra to visit Fr. MacFarland, SJ, who was in Kaduna when I was in Zaria. He really was the source of S. Sharon coming to Nigeria when she did.

Peg and I took a night flight out of Accra to Lagos. The airport was so overcrowded, it was unbelievable! Because British Airways had withdrawn flights from Nigeria, all their customers were trying to take Ghana Airways – and we just didn't fit! Well, chaos reigned, but we reached Lagos safe and relatively sound at 11:30 p.m. We found what was called a "Marriott Hotel" and checked in. The next day was Sanitation or Clean-up, so we got a late sleep (no one can move outside until after 10 a.m..; they are cleaning up their compounds!) We managed to get home by around 5 or 6 p.m..

From there, I got on a merry-go-round. After a few days in Mkar to unpack, check out what the world was doing over here, contacting the architect and such, I went to Jos to deliver some information, gather some, change money, and contact someone. I foolishly thought I would do it in 3 or 4 days, but had to stay 10. After coming back to Mkar to touch base, I went down to Akwa Ibom with a similar list of "things to do." That took just 3 or 4 days and then the driver, Goddy, drove us to Benin City. After one full day, I had seen the people I needed to see and continued on to Lagos. There I worked on a visa, tickets to Ghana, visiting Embassies and a few friends. When I got back to Mkar finally, most of September was gone. Since then I've continued trying to work with the architect and supervisor of the project to move things along. When I get back in mid-October, we will try to begin work on an underground sedimentation/storage tank for rainwater. We received a grant from the Irish Embassy for about $6,000 for this. We have also been down-sizing the plans for the convent to fit the grants we have received for that – a total of $65,000.00. We finished that a few days ago, so new plans are being drawn now. A few other things need to be done, but we'll be starting on the convent soon.

We have had a problem with the "ate" in the front of the school which also needs attention. The weight of the rain and the wind have caused problems with the roof shifting and this in turn is causing cracks in the wall. It looks like we will have to remove the tile roof and follow the wisdom of the people around us – have a roof of grass which comes down low enough to keep out the wind and rain and is much lighter in weight. Another expense not budgeted for!

The school enjoys a wonderful popularity. Folks are forever asking us why we do not have boarding facilities, because many want to come. From the 27 girls in the Remedial Class of last year, 20 were promoted into JSS I. That is such good news! Now if they can just work hard and keep up, we will have achieved our goal. These gals had fallen through the cracks of the faltering educational system here, so they now have a new lease on life. We also have a little evening literacy program going through one of our teachers, and 5 girls from there were able to get into the Remedial Class. That's called redemption! These little kiddos who cannot pass the regular entrance exam are from the immediate surroundings; most are in our own parish of St. Peter. I'm sure that Marie Greenewald, who enabled us to give birth to this school, is rejoicing in heaven! We are rejoicing!

All the hard work of last year to control the erosion has paid off for us this year. It's not perfect, but it's a thousand times better. We have planted our Vetiver grass in the worst places, but we have grass all around, – where there was mud, stone and erosion. We seem to be moving like a turtle, but we are moving! And for that we thank God!

Please help us thank God for all that has been accomplished, and continue to pray for all we need to reach the end of this mighty work.

With love and prayers,
S. Gabe

(Postscript)

Hi!

Please be sure to include Joe in my greetings. How is he doing? And Lois Schioffino?

Lots of love,
Florence

Letter Fifty-two

Notre Dame, Mkar
P.O. Box 501 Gboko
Benue State, Nigeria
29 December 1997

Dear Family and Friends,

My greetings to each of you! I've been composing this letter in my head for ages, but only now am I sitting down to put thoughts on paper. After my leisurely stay in Ghana, I returned to Nigeria only to find myself in the fast lane again! I fell and sprained my ankle; I had malaria and got a reaction to the Lariam I took to get rid of it (I couldn't walk straight!). I thought I was walking under a black cloud. However, things have calmed down a bit for me, so I will try to catch up with you!

Our SSND Community changed its composition. Peg and I are still here, but Regina and Bessie both went to Akwa Ibom. Two new members joined us – Anastasia and Irene. Ann teaches music and CRK (Christian Religious Knowledge); Irene teaches math. Both of them are Ishan by tribe, from Edo State. We're doing fine together, whether working or praying or playing!

School seems to be doing fine. We have 3 classes: Remedial, JSS 1 (2 sections) and JSS 2 (2 sections). The reputation of the school continues to grow, and people keep asking when we will take in boarders. We keep saying our school is a day school and we hope to get a bus someday.

Trying to get things going on the site has been hard. I have not been "steady," which means I'm here a bit, then off to a meeting, back for a bit, then off again. There is very little money to try to get things done in school. We have a major repair problem with the "ate" which everybody loves so. The wind has caused the roof to shift, which caused cracks in the wall. Finding an affordable way to fix it seems to overchallenge everyone. The contractor is "out of money" and Lobi Bank still has what remains of ours. I do the usual "running up and down" to check at Lobi Bank, but I hear promises, promises. I just thank God the bank has not collapsed totally; we can still hope to get something, someday.

In the meantime, we have a grant from the Irish Embassy for a sedimentation tank. It was about $3,000 short of what we asked for, so we can't finish it completely. However, it is mostly finished, and I'm hopeful that God will surprise me somehow. We have a big problem with mud from the borehole from the end of the rainy season until the next rains. It could hurt the pumps and makes a lot of extra work for us, cleaning out the storage tanks, cleaning our water filters, etc. The sedimentation tank will help relieve that and provide some extra storage space for water.

We also have three grants toward the convent. We had to scale down the original plans 2 or 3 times, but we still have a nice plan. To save money, we bought a second hand block-molding machine, which I am assured is a very good make. After some thousands of naira in repair and servicing, we began our own blockmaking before Christmas. The blocks look great and are quite strong, but another part needs servicing. So the site is quiet until the new year. We also bought a small, second hand cement mixer. The better to mix the concrete, I was told. This has been an unbelievable headache, with the mixer down again for about the sixth time. On the positive side, I've been fortunate in getting enough cement to start the foundation of the convent as soon as enough blocks are made. I've ordered and payed for the roof tiles, so they are being made. I can pick up the first batch in January, so I'm told! Our carpenter bought wood for the door and window frames, so this is now drying.

We had two truckloads of cement delivered this morning (380 bags). You need to see all the men, young and old, appear to carry the bags of cement on their heads, offloading it to our store. The standard pay is N5.00 per bag, and most carried 10 bags from each trip. They were so very happy for the work!

We are still having harmattan, that is to say, we are in the dry season. No rain, lots of dust off the Sahara, hazy skies (from the dust), coughs, sneezing, headaches, etc. (from the dust), I'm sure everybody's lungs and sinuses are heavily "dusted." It's hard to keep clothes clean because everywhere is dusty. When I take a shower or wash my hair, the water comes off brown. Personally, I like the rainy season!

We are drawing on our water source plenty because of the building we are doing. Cement blocks have to be watered every day, twice a day, for a week. The new sedimentation tank will be connected to a rain gutter which we will install on part of the school roof to "harvest" the rain. Water, water everywhere, but never where you want it:! We just had to put a pipe line down to carry water to the new convent site. We have a well on that side, but it is on the lower side of the hill and, of course, the water refuses to flow up. I guess we will have to build another overhead tank on that side of the hill. If anyone ever asks you what we would like for Christmas, please tell them water! A steady supply of clean water!

I could rattle on about the building, but I won't. It is only part of my life. A good part of life has to do with SSND matters. We had a Leadership Team meeting here in Nigeria last month. Leaders from Ghana, Kenya, and Sierra Leone, along with our District Leader came. That was really exciting! They wanted to see all of the houses where our Sisters lived and the places where they worked. Planning that was a challenge because of the distances in between our houses. However, the meeting went well. The Leadership Team met everyone (SSNDs), saw their ministries, and were entertained by cultural groups in each place.

There are Area Meetings to plan and attend, Formation Meetings, and other matters that come up that need attention. This past weekend we had 18 young women who are interested in becoming SSNDs here for the weekend. Most are from around this area, but a few had to travel a distance. They were just lovely, and so happy to meet each other. We all enjoyed the time together.

My eye seems to be fine, thank God! I've had it checked once, and the doctor said all was well. He wants me to come back next month for another check.

We had a Christmas party for the school staff and one for our workers. We gave out shirts and jerseys to each of the workers and they were so thrilled. Thanks Jennifer and Carol and whoever else donated clothes! You will be forever remembered! Some of the other clothes that were given to me were given out to the poor and brought a great deal of joy! Some were sold and the money used to replace a collapsed roof and 2 doors of some of the old widows here in Mkar. The Catholic youth did the work.

Some of those who need extra attention are doing well – Janet, a young girl (14) with leprosy is looking fine; Mwuese, age 9, who has a congenital bone problem and was walking on a broken leg, had surgery and is now healing in her POP. When she gets that removed in a couple of weeks, she will get a special shoe and calipers. Sister Irene is going to the Remand Home weekly, and Sister Ann has an special interest in the Orphanage, so I've relaxed from them a bit. The women in the prison are on my agenda for the New Year.

Our life is never dull. Actually, we pray for boredom sometimes, but that prayer has never been answered. We figured we could at least get a good rest, but...

We don't get much mail here, but it could be that no one is writing, just like me. Phone and fax haven't been too steady either. Our own fax number is now 044-470621, in case you want to try it. And we have access to email: mrjohn@gacom.net, in case you want to try that.

People here are praying so very earnestly for God's mercy on this country. Life is very hard and gets harder. The first world is racing ahead while we are sliding backwards at full speed. I do believe that education is the greatest gift we can give to the people here, and our little school is trying. In spite of the financial struggles, we are providing the basics – which are luxuries in other schools (classrooms, teachers, textbooks, desks and chairs,...). God has been good and we are grateful!

Please don't forget us! I never forget you, even though you don't hear from me! Please pray for us, and help us to thank God for all his favors!

With love and prayers,
Gabe

Addendum:

Dear Angie,

Hi, dear friend! How are you? I hope all is well with you and your loved ones!

I'm fine. Moving in the fast lane, but there is a "go slow!"

Lois has pictures I'm sure she'll share with you. Wish I could write more, oftener. I move from deadline to deadline, and just never seem to finish. It must be me!

I'm sure Carolyn will carry news to our "group." Please give them warm greetings for me. I was so sad about Ann H's son Geoffrey. I haven't heard any details as to what happened. A real heart-breaker. Death is a leveler isn't it. Well, Julian says we are "wrapped in God's goodness," and I believe that. There aren't any mistakes on his part.

Take care, Ange. Love to all the Flynns!

Special love to you!
Gabe

Letter Fifty-three

Notre Dame, Mkar
P.O. Box 501 Gboko
Benue State, Nigeria
19 April 1998

Dear Family and Friends,

My warmest greetings to each of you! I have been thinking of you at different times and in so many different ways. Getting thought to reach the paper is always my challenge. One of my latest frustrations is that the memory in my word processor doesn't work anymore. That means I have to type and print at the same sitting. If the power doesn't go off, that's fine, but sometimes the power goes off. Then I lose it all. Trying to have the conveniences of the "First World" while still living in the "Third" where the infrastructures are not steady, if there at all, is a great exercise in patience.

Anyway, it is only 9:30 pm, so I will try to get at least a page finished and print it quickly. I think there is probably dust in my word processor – that's just a guess. And I don't know anyone who can clean it. Many of you have asked about the weather and what effect El Nino has had on us. Well, we have had a very, very harsh harmattan. It was longer than usual, drier than usual and hotter than usual. We all sweat so much we have stopped urinating! We drink water and drink water and drink water. We thank God for cold water, but that runs out fast, believe me. Yesterday we had a "heavy shower" with lots of wind and a little bit of thunder and lightning. Today the sky was blue and the air cool. We could see the Cameroon mountains. By afternoon the sky was white and it was hot. Everything is so dry and thirsty, though there are many things growing that are still green. A marvel! Almost everything we have that was made of wood cracked or bent from the dryness. Doors couldn't close properly, sometimes couldn't even be locked because they had shrunk so much. I'll bet you feel thirsty just reading this, don't you?!

I've had to travel a good deal, as usual. Two weeks ago I went to the Cameroons with Sister Doreen to visit one of our affiliates and meet her family, parish priest, etc. The road joining Nigeria and Cameroons at Ikom is 2 to 3 hours of the worst road you can imagine. And our taxi broke down and we had to sit on the side of the road in the afternoon heat with the gnats for 2 1/2 hours. The road looked like chocolate icing that had been driven over by a Mack truck, – and hardened! Deep, deep gorges made by heavy trucks, almost the height of a car. And some bends and hills; imagine sitting 7 in a small taxi going 60 mph and you've got the picture! Once we were there, we enjoyed ourselves even though it was 100° in the shade. The influence of the French on the food is nice, though we were only there 2 days. Lovely French bread, and abundant, inexpensive chocolate "spread" for bread among others!

You probably have heard the Pope came to visit us and declare Cyprian Tansi "Blessed." There is no way I could ever relay to you the joy, enthusiasm, and excitement that these people had for such a visit. There is no other figure in the world who would get such a welcome. Millions of people travelled to see the Pope, even though petrol was scare and expensive, even though they could hardly see him. We American SSNDs didn't go – the crowd and accommodation are too much for us. But the Nigerian Sisters were thrilled! His presence somehow said Nigerians were still somebody in the eyes of the Pope, even though the rest of the world acts as if they do not exist. And that they have a Blessed Tansi said the same – something good can come out of Nigeria. I understood the organization for the event, part in Onitsha and part in Abuja, was beautifully organized. Everything went smoothly and well.

On the construction site, we have had our share of challenges. Cement has become scarce and expensive. Since we are making our own blocks, the result of this is that the supervisor and/or I "chase" cement at the depot of the cement company (just near Gboko here in Benue State). You try to get there early and get into the manager's office to explain your need, then hope he will give you an allotment. Two months ago we asked for 800 bags. The manager gives us 50 bags at a time, if we get it at all. After you are given the golden piece of paper, you pay for the cement in cash. Our largest denomination is a 50 naira note, but many times the bank has only 20 naira notes to give. So you sit and wait for the accountant to count 20,000 naira. Then you leave and go hire a truck to carry your allotment, pay for the on-loading and follow the truck home. There, you pay for the transport and the off-loading. This little process, added to long hours of waiting and hoping, probably occupies a third of my time. If you think I am doing exciting things, let me tell you – I'm not.

We had a grant from the Embassy of Ireland for an underground tank to collect rain water and serve as a sedimentation tank. The day we tried to fill it to test the pump for sending the water to the overhead tanks (about a month ago), our borehole collapsed. We called the well digger almost immediately to start digging a well, but it is still not finished. That is a long story, but cement for the rings is part of it. We have been buying water since – for the construction as well as for the school and house. And when you make blocks they have to be watered twice a day for 3 or 4 days. On top of that the underground tank began to leak. It took us almost a week to figure out what was wrong. We had to redo the plaster on the inside, and all seems fine now. Right now, cement is so costly in the market that we don't buy it unless we can get it at the depot, which is seldom. So things have slowed down a lot. The foundation and concrete floor are finished. There are 4 different levels because of being on a hill. Some of the steps connecting these are completed, not all. There are 2 courtyards: one for drying clothes and one for enjoying the breezes. Keeping all these level is a marvel because the hill slopes from front down to the back as well as from one side down to the other side. We had just begun to lay out the walls when we had to stop. However, what was done was very well done, so people enjoy coming to look and admire. We may not sleep in the house before the year 2000, but well begun is half done they say. God's time is the best time, so I will patiently try to find out what that is. I need extra time to find extra money anyway.

I will be going to Ghana on the 25th of April for two meetings. Tomorrow I will drive to Jos to do a few things, then fly to Lagos. I need to get my ticket to Ghana and also check on ticket and visa to Kenya for our African assembly in August. In addition I hope to get a laser treatment for my left eye which has become a bit cloudy. Somedays I think I must have milk in my eye, the vision is so poor. This is not the eye that had the detached retina. Rather, it is an opaqueness resulting from cataract surgery a few years back in my left eye. The doctor said the laser will correct it quickly and simply. I pray so! I will be staying with Shola

Robinson in Ikeja while I do the running around, which will be very nice. We are good friends and I feel very much at home in her house. If there is time, I will visit a few embassies and do some "professional begging."

We are 18 in the country now: 8 expatriates and 10 Nigerians. We miss Sister Sharon a lot and pray she can come back soon. We would love to have some more finally professed Sisters to help us with Formation and to flesh out our communities. The expatriates who are here are not young. That the whole project works is proof that it is God's work. I know the political situation probably scares people off. The "transition" is supposed to be complete by October, so we pray God will surprise us with something great! There are a good number of girls interested in coming to join us still. Because of the changes in the Formation program, none will be accepted until 1999.

There is abundant life and abundant struggle here. The poor are suffering more and more. They can't afford to live properly, and they can't afford to die – the expenses are too great for the family. But many do die. The harsh harmattan brings more meningitis, asthma, coughs; poor water brings typhoid and a host of other problems. But let me tell you, these people love life. They know how to celebrate with song and dance, and they laugh much more than you or I. And they pray. They pray and pray and pray. They fast, they keep vigil, they are at Mass in huge numbers. So while they need our help in some ways, they are evangelizing us in others. It is great that God helps us to live together. We're all poor and yet we are all so very rich.

For all the birthdays and anniversaries I've missed, let me wish everyone the choicest blessings God has up his sleeve! I so enjoy hearing what goes on in each one's life! And let me also thank those who have sent gifts of money or other thoughtful things for me to enjoy! I am really so very grateful for your generosity. And thanks too for all the letters, even though my own are so few.

Maybe I'll get chance to write some personal notes on this journey – I'll be on the road for a month.

All the little flying creatures that come out after the first rains are getting pesky. I will sign off now. I wish you all well, and I thank you for remembering me and supporting me and the work we try to do. Please pray for all of us here, and be assured of your own remembrance in our prayers!

With love and prayers,
Gabe

Addendum to letter:

Dear Lois and Carolyn,

Hi! Thanks so much for your letters and all the thoughtful gifts. They are lovely! Eifel Tower completed by Peg already!

This is original copy of my general letter. Other copies are poor. Ruth may need a better copy in order to reproduce it. Could you check?

I finally got the Panasonic snaps. They are lovely! My own camera had died, so I am without pictures for a while.

Please greet everyone for me!

Lots of love.
Florence.

Letter Fifty-four

2 May 1998

Dear Ange,

Hi, dear friend! I hope all is still well with you! I've received your two lovely letters – THANK YOU so much! Perhaps by now the last "general" letter has reached you.

At the moment, I am in Ghana. The formation personnel from the various countries came together for a conference, and the Leadership Team was there. The formators were trying to compare policies for the different stages of formation and work out common ones. They worked hard.

We are in Cape Coast, very near the ocean. It is hot and humid and because the rains are so late, poor Ghana has no water in its reservoir – the source of its electricity! So water and light are scarce everywhere. We managed quite well though – the place where we held the meeting had a big underground tank still full of last year's rain water. We had to be careful, but we're all used to that.

One of our Canadian Sisters who is with us in Nigeria (age 71) got cerebral malaria and almost died. It seems to have affected her heart somehow. I've been really anxious about her. Sr. Peg called and said she gave blood for her and she is now discharged from the hospital. I have another meeting here, so I won't be home for almost two weeks.

I'm glad for these two free days between the meetings. I seldom have time during the day to do things for myself and at night I'm too tired. We had a good rain 2 days ago and a cool breeze today, so I am enjoying writing to you!

It is so good to read of all your wonderful family happenings! I'm so happy for you. Even Michael is making progress, however, slowly or painfully! Enjoy each experience, Ange, and savor it!

The construction of the new convent is so slow because we can't get cement, or if we can, the cost is so high. And then the water problem – our collapsed borehole! God's time is the best time, so I try to be patient. The students are doing well, and we thank God for that. Our foundress said "All God's works proceed slowly and in pain, but then the roots are sturdier and the flowers lovelier."

Please give my greetings and love to everyone! Stay well, Ange, and continue to be your beautiful self! Your friendship is so precious to me!

With lots of love,
Gabe

Letter Fifty-five

9 June 1998

Dear Lois,

Hi! Greetings to you and to all!

After about 2 months mostly on the road for meetings or other business, I'm finally "steady" here at Mkar – at least for a few weeks! I did see the email asking for a student of ecology or someone to communicate with students in Baltimore. Sorry that I just didn't have a chance to investigate the possibilities, and it is probably too late for this school year. However, I will ask around in case there is still interest for future. It costs money to send or receive email and a student might not be able to afford that, but I will inquire all the same.

I've been trying to bring order out of the chaos on my desk – AND file cabinet AND chair! There are forms to fill, including one that needs the date of Daddy's death. Could you send me that? Many thanks! Also, I filed a Durable Power of Attorney for the Motherhouse. A copy will probably be coming to you and Robert. It gives P of A to the provincial, Jane Burke, or her successor or representative in case of terminal illness/accident.

Rain has come, thank God, along with more erosion problems. Though we keep up as best we can, until all the gutters are finished and stone-pitching completed, erosion will be there. Money problems loom large, but I can't get an ulcer because of it. Sure as I solve one problem, two more germinate!

Sister Doreen (Canada) got off smoothly to return to Canada after having cerebral malaria – perhaps Sharon filled you in. I can relax a bit finally!

Please give lots of love to everyone. My word processor is still down, but I hope to write a general letter soon.

Lots of love,
Florence

Letter Fifty-six

Notre Dame, Mkar
P.O. Box 501 Gboko
Benue State, Nigeria
14 June 1998

Dear Family and Friends,

My greetings to each of you! I pray all is well for everyone there as you look forward to the summer months and the change of pace and activities. We are doing fine here, trying our best.

The rains have begun, for which we thank God. They were late this year, so our world was very thirsty! Everything is so lovely and green now! And our site is especially lovely and peaceful, thank God!

Sister Doreen, with whom I travelled to Cameroon, got very sick just at Easter time with cerebral malaria. She is 71 and had stopped taking her malaria preventative medication. (It was Lariam which makes some of us sick to the stomach and causes our eyes to feel funny.) Thanks to God and a wonderful Doctor from Jos Teaching Hospital, Sister recovered. (Most people who get cerebral malaria here, die!) Doreen was due for home leave, so she left as planned at the end of May. However, Sister Virginia Brien accompanied her as far as England, where she stopped to get a good checkup at the Tropical Medical Centre there. Our SSNDs from the Canadian Province are in England, and Doreen is from the Canadian Province. So it was nice that there were folks whom she knew there to meet her and help her navigate in the big city! By now she is at home resting.

We are expecting Sister Sharon back in mid-July and we are looking forward to that. We had also expected an SSND who is interested in coming from the Wilton Province to come for a visit, but she has been unable to get a visa. One of our Japanese SSNDs is hoping to come to teach in Jos, but we cannot get her a visa because we have not been able to clarify the particular job she will be doing. She wants to teach in the Major Seminary in Jos, but there is no opening in the field she wants to teach in.

Trying to communicate out of Nigeria has been almost impossible. It isn't easy to communicate inside either, but when that fails I can at least get in the car and go where I need to. It has been equally difficult for people to get messages in to Nigeria. At least part of the problem is the electric storms that cause damage to lines and equipment. It takes long to repair such things because of "no money" or "no transportation" or "no supplies" etc. Government agencies function like a feeble old man!

Our borehole collapsed some months ago, so we have been buying water a lot. The underground tank collects rain water, but the rains are still infrequent yet. We are having a well dug to replace the borehole, but the well digger is hard to keep track of. We had a small land war going on nearby, and it seems the well digger was organizing the defense lines. I think the well must be 15 feet or so deep by now, with the concrete rings in place. There needs to be a cement lip at the surface and we can connect the water to our system. We practice patience!

Fuel has been hard to get and very expensive. That isn't new. It has affected the functioning of the cement factory, which apparently uses oil for something. So cement is hard to find and it has doubled and tripled in price. We still "chase" cement two or three times a week, but we have virtually stopped work on the convent.

After moving about for most of April and May for meetings and other business, I came back to take a serious look at the coming erosion attractions. We are putting in small (4 inch) diagonal gutters across the road which comes down from the entrance gate to the staff house to get that under control. Since we've been here on the site, we have had a major repair of that road done at the end of every raining season, – hard manual work done by our laborers.. By God's grace it will be successfully under control on that section of road by the end of this raining season!

The steep hill behind the underground water tank looked like a disaster area. The water off that part of the roof runs along the building, which it not yet finished and has no gutters, so it is dangerous. The workmen have hunted and carried hundreds of laterite stones, done the stone pitching, carried and shoveled dirt to cover these and planted trees and bushes. Major work! Next week they plant grass.

We are still trying to terminate the contract on the school in order to finish it ourselves. (We have never regained the 25,000 dollars we lost when Lobi bank crashed, so we are not able to pay the contractor any more money.) It has been almost impossible to get our architect to come here to help us settle this procedure – he is working in Abuja and Kaduna mostly. He has become famous because of our school! In the meantime, there are problems that have developed from the rains because of certain things that are unfinished. So we had to put our attention there lest we suffer additional loss. I think this is what they call crisis management!? Anyway, gradually, gradually, we are able to do some permanent corrections where erosion is concerned. When people come in, what they see is "beautiful." The problems are hardly noticed.

Peg is getting ready for the next class to come in. We will have JSS 1, 2 and 3 next school year, plus Remedial, of course. We have finally gotten our C. of O., (Certificate of Occupancy) so Peg can continue her work on the certification of the school with the Benue Ministry of Education. At long last!

Our house here in Mkar will be closed in August because Peg and I will attend the African District Assembly in Kenya and Irene will be on retreat and holiday. Peg will proceed home for her leave for three months after that.

No doubt you have heard that our Head of State, Abacha, died of a heart attack. God is great! We are now praying that we have not come out of the frying pan into a fire. Nothing has changed much, and we have heard no word from our new leader. The politicians will determine the next chaos.

With love and prayers,
Gabe

Letter Fifty-seven

18 June 1998

Dear Lois and Carolyn,

Hi! How are you doing? I hope all is well! Thanks for your last letters – I'm always glad to hear what is going on there.

I'm enclosing a general letter. Yours is the original copy – the only good one. If you can replace the photocopies with better ones in the envelopes for Ruth and Dorothy Hunt, I'd be glad.

Also enclosed is an email for Jennifer Kovolski, which I was unable to send. The Judge is in the States until mid-July, so I have no access to email. I wish I had known he was going; he could have carried mail for us!

Also enclosed is the magazine from St. Augustine Major Seminary, Jos. The young man for whom you bought the keyboard is sending it – Adamu Konat. [Editor's Note: See letter of 3 December, 1995.]

Finally, there is an envelope for our Provincial, Sr. Jane Burke. Could you post it or drop it of at 6401 for me? Many thanks!

Please give my love to everyone. How is Lois Schiaffino? Please send my greetings to her.

Lots of love,
Florence

Letter Fifty-eight

Notre Dame, Mkar
P.O. Box 501 Gboko
Benue State, Nigeria
20 September, 1998

Dear Family and Friends,

My greetings to each of you! I hope all is well with each one, and that you are enjoying whatever you are doing, and whatever events and celebrations are taking place in your family circles. Another autumn is rolling around, lest we forget that time is passing steadily, and life is a process, not a state of being!

We are fine here, thank God. Peg is home on leave until early November. We have two new members in our community here at Mkar, one a professed Sister, Priscilla, and one a postulant, Florence, who is here just for one term. We are expecting another Sister, Dorothy, soon, so our house will be full. Dorothy is having surgery down in Akwa Ibom and so will recuperate there.

We are still in the raining season, so we have the beautiful majestic skies that I love. We also have erosion, but we are getting to be quite good at checking it. However, it is costly and eats into our budget!

Our third year of school began very well with the V.P., Father Kajo, at the helm. The girls seem ever so happy to come to Notre Dame; I pray the fruits of their educations and training will make us all proud and happy. At the end of this academic year, the girls in JSS 3 will take an exam. This will be an opportunity for us to see how they perform in comparison to students in other schools. As the students increase, the staff of course increases.

You may remember that last year our borehole collapsed. We had a well dug to replace it. For various reasons, it took so long to complete. It is functioning now, thank God! As usual, at the end of the raining season the water becomes muddy. Water flows down through the soil in the hill and gets into the well (or borehole). I seem to spend my life moving the elements – trying to get water where it is not, trying to stop water from coming where it is, moving laterite stone, moving earth, …

The convent is not quite up to the lintels. We ran out of money so I am trying to look around for some other sources. I tell people that I am now a professional beggar! We are hoping to finish up to the lintel level before the rains stop, to save us watering the blocks – moving water, again! I've learned not to worry about the innumerable problems that keep popping up. I move from crisis to crisis, deadline to deadline, and wait on God to do the rest. We received a gift of 100 bags of cement last week, which was a tremendous help to us. I guess it will all eventually get finished – in God's own time.

There is a friend of ours in Baltimore studying at St. Mary's Seminary/University. He is Father Daniel Melaba, a young priest of the Makurdi Diocese. He was a wonderful neighbor to Peg and me when we first came to Gboko. All those months we lived at St. John's, he checked on us, said Mass in English for us most days, helped us pack up the truck when we had to travel, and unpack when we came back. He was always there with a smile and a willing hand to help. I hope those of you who can will help us return his hospitality by making yourselves known to him and inviting him to share a slice of life with you somehow. I did give him some addresses/phone numbers, and I know Peg is there for awhile, but it is hard to be a stranger in a strange land! If you can, please help to make him feel welcomed!

We had our first District Assembly in Kenya, a great experience for all of us who were able to attend. We were in Kenya at the time of the bombing of the American Embassy, but in fact, we had left Nairobi to travel to Kisii on the day it happened. When we stopped for lunch, we heard the tragic news on CNN. Sister Roxanne, the Novice Director, and the novices joined those who sorted through the rubble, separating out the glass and looking/listening for survivors. As the events unfolded, the papers were filled with pathetic pictures and stories. There were real heroes on the scene, working round the clock. Violence! How we all hate it!

There are a number of meetings coming up, both within Nigeria and outside – Ghana, The Gambia. I am a rolling stone, gathering no moss. Getting ourselves organized well is vitally important, so none of us minds the overtime. My aging brain sometimes feels overloaded, with a short circuit now and again, but otherwise, I'm O.K. I think!

We are having the Final Profession of our first African SSND on 14 November, 1998. That will be a big event for all of us. Sister Bernadette Amimi will take her final vows in her home parish. Shortly after that she will begin her studies for her degree at the University of Calabar. Please keep her in your prayers!

My plan is to get copies of this letter into a DHL that I will send to Sister Marie Antoinette from Calabar on Monday. I won't have time to add personal notes, so I hope you will excuse me. I am really so very grateful for notes from you. I look forward to hearing news from all of you!

Please take care, stay well, and find joy wherever you are! Thanks for all your love and support!

With love and prayers,
Gabe/Florence

Letter Fifty-nine

Notre Dame, Mkar
P.O. Box 501 Gboko
Benue State, Nigeria
25 November 1998

Dear Family and Friends,

My greetings to each and every one of you! As I look at today's date, I realize I should say Merry Christmas and Happy New Year to you as well! I pray that everyone is well, and for those in my generation bracket, growing old gracefully!

Many thanks for the newsy letters and monetary gifts that came back with Peg. It is always so good to hear from you and catch up on life over there in the fast lane. I'm sorry I missed Bob's wedding, but I know he will fill me in whenever I get there.

Our weather is a bit confused here. We seem to be in a limbo with the sky showing signs that there is moisture up there, but we've had no rain for almost a month. However, the harmattan has not come either. It is hot and the ground is already getting hard. This is the time for the orange harvest here – when the rains have stopped. They are abundant and their juice is very sweet. They are cheaper now, so we have the luxury of orange juice! Poinsettias have been in bloom for several weeks already (they grow on bushes and even trees here), and the lovely pink "Christmas rose" is also out. That grows on a small tree with grey bark, but the leaves come out only when the flower is ready to die. We have many lovely, different types of grasses here, some of which are quite high by now. Those that have gone to seed may be a dusty rose or greyish white. They "sweet" my eye, as they say here. This is the time young boys come out with long sticks to beat the grass looking for field mice – a real delicacy, we are told. Sometimes the grasses are burned to drive the mice into the waiting hands of their hunters – and houses get burned! Anyway, the signs of the season's change are all around us, even though it is not completed.

Our community is five now: Peg, Irene, Priscilla, Florence (a postulant) and myself. Florence will be leaving in a couple of weeks for her home leave, and then she will return to the Postulate. She has been here for 3 months apostolic experience, working mostly with the Remedial class in Peg's absence. Peg is just back from her home leave, but jumped right into the thick of things. Irene is in her 2nd year with us as math teacher and doing very well; Priscilla has just come to join us from the Jos community. She has opened up the Guidance Office for the school. Dorothy will be joining us from one of the communities in Akwa Ibom, but she is still recuperating from surgery. And as for me, I'm not sure what I'm doing!

Our BIG EVENT was the celebration of final vows by Bernadette Amimi, Bern is our first finally professed SSND from Africa, so we in Nigeria feel very privileged. We all went down to Calabar for the occasion. Some of the Sisters from Kenya and Ghana joined us, so it was very, very special! We had said in the celebration that community is the sign by which we want to be known, so at the end, all the finally professed SSNDs came up, stood around Bern, prayed for her, then blessed her: Bernadette, we commend you to the Holy Spirit, through the powerful intercession of the blessed Virgin Mary, and we entrust you forever into her blessed hands. Remember that blessing? SSNDs used to bless their children at the end of each school day with that formula.

After the festivities, I went to Port Harcourt airport with the Ghana group to see them off, then took the Kenyans around to see the houses in Akwa Ibom. I accompanied them to Lagos since it was their first time flying and their first time in Nigeria.

Sisters Jane Burke and Joan Maier are coming for a visit from Baltimore – Jane's first time to Nigeria!. They fly into Kano tomorrow, so Sharon will meet them and drive with them down to

Jos to begin their visits with us and the long journey toward the south. I'll go up to Jos with Goddy (the driver) on Saturday to bring them to Mkar for a day or so, then they will go down to Akwa Ibom to visit the four houses there. I pray the heat and the travel doesn't debilitate them too much. We would love to have them enjoy their visit. Joan always came faithfully when she was our Councilor, but that has been long since – 3 years?

All this travel has become a part of life for me, with lots of meetings in between – more travel. Petrol is still a problem for us over here: scarce and expensive. The only thing more frustrating than travel is communication! But we keep on keeping on. We act like we are living in the first world, when, in fact, we are definitely not there.

I now have a laptop, equipped with everything needed for email, a Windows 98. It took me 2 days to find an adapter to receive the American plug on it. The laptop doesn't need a transformer, but the printer does. As I was strangling myself amid the wires, I put the printer into the adapter instead of the transformer and blew the small transformer on its wire. It took me about 3 weeks to get someone to fix that. I have now begun computer lessons, since I can't understand what I am being told to do by the machine. I've been trying to register for the email, but the only phones that I can use to make international calls – and register – are in Makurdi. I thought all this technology was supposed to be a saving of something! Time? I don't think so! Money? Not really! Trying to live the first world in the third world is like putting a round peg in a square hole!

My teacher told me that the computer I have is the Mercedes Benz of the computers. I told him he was looking at someone who rides a tricycle! But I will keep on keeping on.

Our new convent is up to the lintels and looking good. We are waiting for some more money to flow our way. In the meantime, our new well seems to be having problems. Not enough water. As we are about to enter the dry season, this is a problem! So the well is going to be dug deeper. Next week, I hope!

School seems to be doing very well. The girls are happy as larks to come each day, even though many trek long distances. Going home in the afternoon heat, when they are hungry is the hardest, I think. Our school is almost certified with the government. We had the inspection visit last month, and seem to have passed the test. We are waiting for the letter of approval. At the end of JSS 3, our students will take a National Examination. We would like them to be able to take it here so it is properly supervised, but we must be certified for that. So we wait in joyful hope! The first JSS exam will be around June. 1999.

Most people seem happy with what our new leader, Abubakar, has done so far. There are still some big problems that need to be addressed, but his time is too short to solve all the problems. One problem is this petrol "scarcity" that is always followed by abundant black market petrol. It is anywhere from 4 to 10 times the legal price, sometimes contaminated with kerosene or something to dilute it. The corruption that is everywhere is like a cancer. I don't know how it can ever be contained, because we have no accountability systems that work here. People are so easily bought off.

Since I began this, Jane and Joan have arrived and so has Dorothy. We are a full house indeed. The school has also received the certification we have been applying for! Halleluiah! And I received more mail and more gifts carried by Jane and Joan. I am rushing to get this letter finished so they can carry it back. Many, many thanks for all the very thoughtful and very generous gifts! You are tremendous when I think of what a poor correspondent I am. Mea culpa! I had thought I would write personal notes at the bottom of this page, but I'm not sure I'll make it. If not, know that it isn't because I've forgotten you. It's because I'm over here trying to put round pegs in square holes!

If all goes well, I will fly to Lagos on Friday to meet up with Jane and Joan. After I see them off, I will work on my visas for the Gambia and Ghana, get my plane tickets, and do a few other things.

With much love to each of you and the promise of prayers!

Gabe
(Florence)

Letter Sixty

Sunday
6 December 1998

Dear Lois, Carolyn and Joe,

Hi! How are you all doing? I haven't heard much about Joe's new job – what you are actually doing?

Carolyn, sorry about Terry! I know that must have been so hard! – and for Lois as well, I'm so grateful to you both for your letters and gifts. I wish I were as faithful.

Lois, I'm sorry to hear about your back problems. I had some pain in my sacroiliac for a while, but exercise has helped. The osteopath said she thinks I have scar tissue adhering to the muscle. Anyway, I'm O.K. and I can function fine. Long hours traveling can set off the pain a bit, but not too much. And the exercises help.

I had an unexpected vacation yesterday in the Hilton Hotel in Abuja. I got stuck on my way to Lagos because I didn't know all the movement was prohibited due to the elections. It was short but sweet – hot bath, TV, air-conditioning, ice cream, brewed coffee, no interruptions – great.

I wanted to see Jane and Joan off tonight, so I'm trying to combine that with some visa/ticket business I have to do for upcoming meetings.

Lois, don't worry about Elizabeth. Her situation is bad, all right, but Sr. Virginia oversees her needs. Even the Bishop helps out. Her paternal uncle is a jerk and wants her off the property – the situation is awkward. We can't control it and can't take Elizabeth out of it. Any time you can send a little wool, she is very happy.

My email buddy, Judge Ikongbeh, was promoted to the High Court and will be moved. I have been in touch with an engineer in Gboko for lessons on a new laptop, but I've not had time to go yet. He is big into computers, too, and has a little school going in the evenings to teach computer.

I had hoped to get off notes to more people, but I didn't. Yesterday I worked on my accounts! Maybe in the next couple of days...

Special greetings to Ann Kelly, Bill Willman, Rose, et. al.

Lots of love,
Florence

Letter Sixty-one

8 December 1998

Dear Ange,

Hi, dear friend! I was so happy to hear from you and hear all the good news! What a blessing to be able to share in the coming of your first grandchild. Deo gratias that all went well – and is still going well.

Thanks, too, Ange for the monetary gift. It helped me pay November salaries. I am hopeful of some money in January, so I will just wait. Once it comes, we will move quickly. We really want to "pack in" to our new home.

At the moment, I am in Lagos, working on a visa for the Gambia and one for Ghana. I have a meeting in Gambia in January and one in Ghana in February. In between there is one back here in Nigeria – barely enough time in between to travel! I saw our two visitors, Jane and Joan, off on Sunday night. I spent yesterday working on the visas, plane tickets, changing money. The harmattan has not yet come, so it is hot and humid. The petrol shortage causes long queues on the streets at the filling stations, which add a little more chaos to the traffic. Although sometimes tempers are short, I marvel at the good dispositions of people!

Jane and Joan were very supportive. It was a boost to have them here. And they are both quick to see problems and understand what is going on. Some problems are hard to explain in letters, and even when you try, they are not understood. Jane also told me there are one or two people interested in coming to Nigeria – that was good news indeed!

I'm sorry to hear Mary Ellen's marriage didn't work out, but I'm glad she is back in the Bible group. Dot has been so good sending letters and other little things, and Erin sends a note now and again. I want to write them a personal note too. Time is my problem. I spend many hours in planes, buses, taxis, but I can't usually write letters then.

What of Ann H? How is she doing? And Danny?

Very shortly I'll be off for my rounds for the day. I'll go where I can make some phone calls and then pick up the visas and check out how I will travel back. In between all this, I've gotten some extra sleep/rest. Last Saturday I was stuck in Abuja, I couldn't move out because of the elections – so I enjoyed the hotel – A.C, hot bath, T.V. – grand!

Ange, did you read *Angela's Ashes* by Francis McCourt? Very touching story about the author's childhood growing up in Ireland in terrible poverty. His father was an alcoholic. I thanked God for your and Mike's courage when I was reading it. What a battle to fight! I thank God for young Mike's courage as well. Praise God for his progress!

Take care, friend! I think of you often!

Lots of love,
Gabe

Letter Sixty-two

Date: 27 May 1999 12:06:36 +0100
From: ssndmkar@infoweb.abs.net
To: lroeder@umaryland.edu
Subject: Greetings

Greetings from Lagos! I am here working on visas for Kenya for one of the young sisters and myself. She is going there in hopes of studying and I am accompanying her. I'll be back in a week or two. I hope everyone is fine there. As it looks, I will not be coming home this year. There is too much going on and I can't find 3 months of uninterrupted time. Maybe early next year...

I now have this "TOP-OF-THE-LINE" laptop computer but hardly manage to use it. It has a modem, but we do not have good phones. My address is ssndmkar@infoweb.abs.net. I'm not even using my own laptop at this moment – I couldn't carry it. I'm at the Infoweb office on Victoria Island to pay in some money. The last time I tried to wire some, it took weeks before it was verified. This was much easier. I wish I had time to email everybody who is on, but there are only 2 computers for customers to use and there are people waiting. Maybe when I'm in Kenya there will be time.

How is Carolyn's new dog? I hope it is working well. Please do give lots of love from me to everyone. I promise a longer letter very soon. Sister Sharon's mom left the money from the sale of her house in Pittsburgh to the project in Mkar, so we have some activity there. We have the Senior Secondary almost ready and we are working on the convent. Hopefully by the time I am back it will be ready for roofing. I've applied for a grant for the roof and I'm hoping a response to that request will also be there when I get back!

Our Junior Secondary received accreditation and permission to be an exam centre. Deo gratias! There is always work to be done on the site, but actually I'm on the road a lot. As we get bigger, life gets more complicated – more meetings, more happenings, more problems. When we get phones ...ha! Life will be so easy! My own phone is still on 4 wheels.

Jos has a phone/fax that works now. That number is 234-73-610185. I'm in touch with Sharon periodically and go up every month or two. She sometimes has a chance to send messages down with someone travelling. We are investing a big sum for a phone in Uyo in Akwa Ibom next fiscal year. We already have the computer with modem which came from the U.S. The mother board has a problem and has to be fixed (replaced?). They also have an E-mail number at the university, but they are on strike. I can't remember that number off hand. Our fax number was changed, but we seldom get faxes because the phone system is so poor. I will check it and send that along too.

How is Catherine Schiaffino doing? Her life must be dramatically different! Please extend love and greetings to her – and Ann Kelly and Bill and Rose etc. I am alive and well.

◄ Gabe with construction staff at Mkar

▲ Almost completed convent, Notre Dame Mkar, July 2001

◄ Beginning of convent construction Mkar, April 1998

1999-2004

Helping to Establish SSND Africa Province

Following the successful launch of the school and the continuing completion of the convent, Gabe traveled more, providing instruction and guidance for the blossoming formation program for African women interested in joining the School Sisters. While at Mkar, she has served as area leader and continued in that role until 2002. Her travels included trips to Ghana and stays in Uyo in southern Nigeria. Her role as a teacher of the women in formation expanded.

A visit home in the summer of 2000 was followed by the unexpected death of Sr. Sharon Dei. After attending the funeral in Baltimore, Gabe sadly returned to Nigeria and settled her affairs, requiring several trips to central Nigeria.

In early 2002, she officially left Mkar and moved back to the southeast region of Nigeria, where she had served in the 1980s. It was at one of the many farewells in Mkar that she was given the title "Mure U Tiv," or "Shade of the Tiv." The touching description of the meaning of this title, found in Gabe's letter of February 12, 2002, gives us some indication of the community's appreciation of the values she lived and their sorrow at her leaving them.

Busy as she was, her interest in everyone who crossed her path is evident in her letters, with vivid descriptions of her fellow sisters, her students, and the needy she saw around her. We have no letters after June, 2004. Gabe returned to the U.S. in 2004 to visit and deal with medical issues. She returned to teach the women in formation at Uyo until her retirement to Villa Assumpta in Baltimore in 2007.

Letter Sixty-three

23 June, 1999

Dear Family and Friends,

My greetings to you all! It has been longer than usual since I've written, and I'm really sorry about that. Clearly, I am not the master of my time – it seems to be the master of me!

I do hope everyone is well, happy and enjoying whatever it is you are doing. I try to stay in that state myself, though I must admit that mostly I just try to do all my "homework" and meet the next deadline whether I am happy or not! My eye that had the surgery for detached retina is doing very well, thanks be to God!

Some of you know that I now have a beautiful laptop computer with a modem for email. After much "running up and down" I have an email address: ssndmkar@.infoweb.abs.net. My one remaining problem is that I do not have a phone that can access the Infoweb. Our phone in Gboko is "analog" and just doesn't work well; the phone is Jos is digital and works sometimes. What everyone is hoping for eventually is IDD – international direct dialing, which works well. Few folks have this, however. Someday! Someday! I found out by accident that when I am in Lagos, I can go to the Infoweb Office on Victoria Island and the access is instant. I can receive or send email. At the moment I am in Jos with my laptop, but there is no access.

This year I have been "on the road" more than ever. I've been to Ghana twice, to The Gambia, to Kenya – and up and down the roads of Nigeria to Jos and Akwa Ibom. There are many exciting things happening for us as a new District. The price of the new life among us is meetings and more meetings, evaluations, drawing up policies, directories, etc. All the clocks and calendars are leaking; there is never any time left over. So I try to enjoy whatever I'm doing, wherever I am. Sometimes it works, sometimes it doesn't.

My last trip outside of Nigeria was to Kenya to accompany one of our Nigerian sisters who is going there to study. Since we have consolidated our two novitiates into one (in Ghana), the building in Kenya is now a House of Studies. There are three sisters there attending Tangaza, a Catholic University set up by the religious of Kenya and run by the Christian Brothers. By God's grace, we will have another Nigerian sister going there in January. By coming together in the Novitiate and the House of Studies, we are hoping that the African sisters will get to know and understand each other better. The bonding process is so important, but so difficult across the big distances we have. Meetings bring us together, but time and heavy agendas limit the "getting to know you" process.

At the end of last year we had our first Final Profession in Nigeria; at the end of this year we hope to have our second, and in March of the year 2000 our third. Slowly, we are growing. As Area Leader, I am responsible for formation – a ministry both very challenging and time consuming, and yet also very encouraging. Our women come from different tribes, so they are counter-cultural in living and working together in love and peace. Their cultural adjustments can be as great as ours. We are all busy with the work of trying to become a province. These past three years of living as a District have been a test of sorts, but also a time of learning and growth. We are evaluating what has been and looking forward to what will be.

Our school at Mkar has received its accreditation from the State for the Junior Secondary School. We have a fine Board of Governors which meets each term. Next year we begin Senior Secondary. We still face many challenges. The last head of Government ordered a very significant increase in wages in the country, which is still not totally in place yet. In spite of that, prices are rising in the market place. Some of those who have not received the wage increase are on strike, teachers included. We have a major problem at Notre Dame, because we have only our tuition to deal with such things, and you don't just raise tuition in the middle of the term. Besides, if we raise it too much, we will lose some of our students. So we are treading water on that issue and praying for a miracle!

Our main road through Mkar and the road from it to our school have been deteriorating badly over the past couple of years. We had expected the main road to be repaired this past January, but... promises, promises. In the meantime, our cars take a terrific beating. The rock and ridges and potholes do a great job on the steering and alignment. Now that the rains have come, the roads will get a little worse. The government is trying to straighten out its money, (our past leaders robbed the citizenry and its treasury of unbelievable amounts of money!) and it is somehow tied up or not available at the moment. Until that problem is resolved and money is released to the road building companies, our road will stay as it is or get worse.

We are still working on the convent at Notre Dame, Mkar. The walls are very nearly finished. Right now we are molding blocks. If all goes well, we will be ready for the roof by the end of July. August is a month of meetings for us, so the site will be quiet. In September I think we can do the roof. Once that is in place, other things can go quickly. We are using the money from the sale of Sister Sharon's mother's house, which was left to the Mkar project. It has taken us far because the exchange rate is good right now. The SSS building is getting in shape for September as well. We still look for grants, fight erosion after every rain, and spend lots of time "chasing cement." (Our workers assure me that I am going to win the battle against erosion! We have more vetiver grass on our site than you can ever imagine. In case you didn't know, vetiver grass helps control erosion; I came to know it here.)

On the political scene, people are really very hopeful. Obasanjo has moved very quickly and decisively in confronting some of the major problems here. He has given people a renewed sense of expectation for something better. I pray for the man every day. He seems to be doing a major house cleaning of the army, and attacking corruption head on! May God give him strength. We really do have wonderful human resources here, now is their time to shine.

If anyone is able to send me some CR-100 carbon tapes for my Canon Word processor, I would be most grateful. They are not to be found here – though I found one. The man asked the equivalent of $25.00 for it. (They cost $5.00!) Trying to straddle the First World and the Third World ain't no fun!

I don't expect to be home this year for leave, and I can't just say when I will come. I will know better in the new year. In the meantime, I wish you all Happy Birthdays, Anniversaries, Jubilees, 4th of July, etc. I am very grateful to those who write even when I don't. I love to read news of you! And even though it is hard for me to sit down and write, I think of you and wonder how you are doing. I wish you God's blessings in abundance, and pray that your life is unfolding gracefully, whether you are young or older.

Will someone see that Father Dan Melaba gets a copy of this letter? Many thanks!

With love and prayers,
Florence Gabe

Letter Sixty-four

OLA Conference Center
Maryland, Lagos
Nigeria
21 October 1999

Dear Family and Friends,

My greetings to each of you! And many, many thanks for your letters and gifts sent with Virginia and Betty. You are wonderful to be so faithful when I am such a lousy letter-writer.

The Leadership Team for the District of Africa just concluded a meeting here at the Conference Center of the Sisters of Our Lady's Apostles in Maryland. Way back in the late 70s, when I first came to Nigeria, we sometimes stayed at the convent next door. Since then, this Center and a Generalate house have been built, one structure on either side of the large convent. The complex is walled off and nicely landscaped, so you almost forget you are on a very busy (and noisy) street. The Center is great for meetings. It is our first time of using it for such, but we felt very relaxed and were able to get all our work finished. The parish church is a 5-minute walk away, also walled off and beautifully landscaped to give a sense of peace and quiet in a really busy area.

The other Team members went to the airport last night, headed for Kenya and Ghana. As usual, I am trying to kill more than one bird with my stone, so I am working on a visa for one of our Nigerian Sisters who will be going to Germany after Christmas for an SSND International Program. Every couple of years there seems to be something to help us celebrate our internationality. Two of our African sisters will be going to this one: one from Nigeria and one from Kenya.

Actually, I had taken all the documents to the Catholic Secretariate last Friday in hopes that I would be able to fly to Akwa Ibom today, but... "The best laid plans of mice and men ..." mostly go awry for me! The young man working on the visa for me got malaria, so he only started on it yesterday. While I was running around Lagos Island, I checked on visa forms for another sister who might be going to Kenya to study, and forms for some of us expatriates for a meeting in Ghana. Of course, when I am that close, I just hop over to Victoria Island and check Infoweb for email. I forgot to bring my email addresses, so I didn't send anything.

I only have to pack tonight. Tomorrow I will go to the airport early and get the first plane to Calabar or Port Harcourt. We have a Formation Team Meeting scheduled for whenever I can get there this weekend. We are very flexible folks here! Either you flex or you get hypertension. From there I go back to Mkar. Hopefully, I will find some of the wood on site for the roof of the convent.

Wood doesn't fare well in Benue because of termites. We are living on their kingdom, and since they were there long before us, we are outnumbered a million to one. So wood has to be sprayed or painted with a chemical before we use it. After the wood frame for the roof is on, we will put the Benco tiles – like the ones on the staff house and the school. Our effort to support the local industry! They are beautiful and cool. They are also heavy, so the framework is terribly important. We had to learn some painful and expensive lessons when we built the school, but we think we have.

At any rate, it is good to see some progress on the convent. We are anxious to get into it. Our community fills the duplex house and we feel "split" being in two apartments. Money is mostly the problem in getting finished, but we keep on trying! In between meetings, that is! The convent is big. It has 9 bedrooms plus 2 guestrooms, a community room and a workroom in addition to the parlor, dining room and a big kitchen (thank God), a chapel, a laundry room, an ironing room, a toilet/bath room and 2 courtyards (1 for laundry and I for relaxation). We are already 5 sisters in the community. We still have work to do on the secondary school yet, so our hands are full. We still have to complete some of the labs and paint. We are also feeling pinched that we do not have any place to assemble the children (almost 300 now), nor do we have a dining area for them. And then there is the constant plea for hostels to allow the students to board! We thank God that the school is doing well and enjoying a good reputation.

We have been working really hard on becoming an African Province. That is a big part of the reason for so many meetings. We have lots of work to do, so we are asking for a 3 year extension as a District. Our General Superior attended our last District Assembly in Ghana and was very encouraging to us. It seems our sisters in Central and South America are in a similar process. Everybody is restructuring! Our population is changing as well with the entrance of Africans and Asians into the Congregation.

As you can imagine, we are very happy with Obasanjo. His work is monumental, but he seems to be trying. The stories that are coming out about Abacha are so sickening, I could cry. We were all afraid of him, but no one dreamed he was so demonic! And the money he stole from these people! The amounts of money he put into bank accounts outside this country is obscene. The changes just can't be felt fast enough by the poor. They suffer terribly. They can't afford to live and they can't afford to die. Funerals are very expensive here because the bereaved family has to feed everybody who comes.

The U.S. is promising to help Nigeria. I hope they don't use the help as a means to control the country for its own ends. There are signs of hope around, but basically, most things still don't work well where I live. The school system needs gigantic help on every level, the health system, water, roads, employment, etc., etc., etc.

We had good rain this year, so we can hope for a good harvest, though farmers complain of no fertilizer. I'm sorry you all had such a bad year for rain. Here, almost everybody is a farmer, including us, so poor rain is killing.

There are young boys around the site all the time looking for work to pay school fees or buy books or clothes. We try to utilize them as much as we can, but we just can't help everyone. And there are always poor people coming with emergency needs. Our own workers ask for advances on their salaries for facing troubles, or extra work. So life is still tough amid the signs of promise!

As it looks now, I will be getting my home leave sometime in May of 2000. We have a Formation Conference in Kenya the end of April into early May, so after I return to Nigeria, I will head toward Baltimore. It will be good to see everyone again.. I hope we haven't changed too much! But I think you will recognize me.

Caitlin Brune is in Kenya at the moment, soon to go to Ghana. We were expecting her to come here to Nigeria, but she just wrote to say she will do that some time in the future. Her funds are running low.

31 October 1999

Happy Halloween, everyone! I am back at Mkar. We are getting ready for some guests who are coming to help us reflect and remember our beginnings and our history here. This is part of our celebration of our 25th Jubilee of ministering in Nigeria, though there were 2 years when one SSND was here. Sister Melmarie is coming over for the occasion.

We had to get a new phone for our line in Gboko at the Nativity Convent. I spent some time yesterday trying to send email, but no luck. I never even got through to a phone at Infoweb. In fact, it took me 30 minutes to get through to Jos. Someday! Someday! We are working on getting a phone in Uyo at our Formation House.

We have a fax with a modem and we even have an email number ready. When the phone is connected it should be great. We were told they are getting digital phones there. However, 'till we see for eye!

When I arrived in Akwa Ibom last week, I found that the convent at Ikot Etuk Udo was attacked by armed robbers. That is the 2nd time in about 4 months; the 3rd time in its history. Needless to say the Sisters were upset. One had just had surgery. We thank God no one was physically hurt.

Back here on the site, the work is going along slowly but surely. The framework for 2 sections is going up; it will probably be finished at the end of the week. Then the tiles will go on. If more wood starts coming tomorrow, it will be treated and ready when the carpenters are ready. The driver Goddy (Godwin) is taking pictures for me.

I'm working on landscaping on the SSS side of the building, and fighting erosion as usual. I now have to choose flowers and bushes that are goat-proof. Our goats roam around and eat what they want – and spoil many things. I have now identified which plants are nice and that the goats don't like, so we are changing some things. The goats are terrible enemies of our fruit trees. When the trees are small, the goats chop all the leaves and kill the tree. We have lost many trees and flowers to goats! This year, I am having all the scrubby wild trees in three sections pulled up while the ground is still soft (we are still getting some rains). Once the rains stop, our ground gets very hard, very fast! Next rainy season we will plant 2 orange orchards and one mango orchard. Hopefully, in a few years this will produce some income for the school. We are having unexpected difficulties with paying salaries because the government increased their teachers salaries (on paper). Almost overnight salaries were doubled! Of course, our teachers want the same, since, as they say, they are all going to the same markets! And we want to do that, but we can't increase tuition that fast without losing the children we came to help. Many teachers have not seen the increase, or they are many months behind in their salary. So we are really sweating it out. The fruit trees will take a few years to produce fruit, but oranges and mangoes have a big market here. Anyone want to plant a few trees?

I'm also thinking of raising pigs. There is a good market for them here and I understand they are prolific – 10 to 15 in a litter! We have to work out estimates and look for funding – if everybody approves of the idea!

I received a mail bag with lots of lovely books from the Motherhouse, but with no name of a sender. Does anyone know who I should thank?

As it looks now, I will be mailing this letter. I pray it doesn't take too long to reach you. Let me say "Happy Birthday" to Ruth! And Happy Thanksgiving and Merry Christmas to everyone, just in case!

(handwritten)

Hi! I hope you are both well! And Joe! And Nevada!

I'm enclosing pictures. If you can copy some or all and send them around, it would be swell! Please be sure a copy goes to S. Jane Burke at the Motherhouse, please!

We have so many little wildflowers amid the grass and the weeds – you would enjoy the colors and the shapes. As we get a few trees, we get birds. Their songs are quite different. Now the country is sane again, maybe you could think of coming over!

Elizabeth was so very happy with her wool! (Virginia looks after her, not me.) She is alive and she is managing.

Lots of love,
Florence

Letter Sixty-five

Date: 9 Nov 1999 10:53:30 +0100
From: ssndmkar@infoweb.abs.net
To: lroeder@umaryland.edu
Subject: Greetings

Hi, Lois, Carolyn, Joe,

Greetings from Lagos! I'm here on some business, so I thought I would say hi. I pray all are well. I'm fine, I think. The buses and taxis in Lagos are on strike because of too much harassment from policemen looking for money, so movement is difficult and slow. But we try! Please greet all. Give Alica a special hug and kiss for her birthday – sorry I missed it.

Letter Sixty-six

From: ssndmkar@infoweb.abs.net
[SMTP:ssndmkar@infoweb.abs.net]
Sent: Tuesday, January 25, 2000 4:04 AM
To: Jroeder@nib.org
Subject: RE: Reply

Hi, Joe!

Yes, I did get your reply. Many thanks! I'm glad to know your work is challenging and satisfying.

I am on this Infoweb line, but my problem is that the phones in Benue are still analog, and the email just doesn't connect with an open line. Certainly not easily! However, people are trying to improve the phones, especially business folks, so we wait and hope. That seems to be the main vocation of people in the developing world.

How I wish there were 1/10 of the opportunities for the blind here that exist over there. Little by little, there has been some change – in attitudes toward the blind and handicapped, and willingness to train or educate them. I understand there is a blind lecturer at Unijos. Patience is the virtue.

I was trying to work on getting a grant for a small project for our school yesterday. I didn't succeed, but was given other names and agencies to try. I want to have a piggery to generate funds for the school. When the government raised the salary of civil servants, our own teachers wanted a raise. However, our salaries come from tuition, and you can't just double that overnight. We increased it some, but not enough to satisfy the teachers. We are afraid of losing the student population, because many are poor – children of small farmers, widows, etc. Some parents are still more than ready to marry off their daughters, so to ask them to invest more money when they will just lose them through marriage anyway is risky. The school is doing very well and has a wonderful reputation so far. We are up to Senior Secondary 1 (10th grade). The pig manure will help me a lot to fertilize our terrible soil, and we can sell the new pigs. People around here like pork, and reproduction is relatively quick. I need $1600 to start. When I get back to Mkar and my computer, I'll try some other places.

We have a cow in addition to our goats and chickens, dog and cat. Her name is Gracey and she is pregnant, thank God. Her task is to help us cut the grass and give us manure.

We grow some a few things like yam, peanuts, guinea corn, maize, leaf, but not lots because the soil is so poor. However, we try.

Joe, do you know how to find out the process for drying tomatoes? We have lots and lots of tomatoes in our area, but there is no way to preserve them. Peg tells me that dried tomatoes are popular in the States. Maybe Carolyn would know. I didn't carry her email number with me this morning though, and I'm flying to Jos this afternoon, by God's grace.

Please greet everyone for me!

Lots of love, Florence

Letter Sixty-seven

20 April 2000

Dear Carolyn and Lois,

Hi! Greetings from Nigeria! And thanks for your long and newsy letter, Carolyn!

I am hoping to be home by 20 May. From Lagos, I'll fly on the 12th to Zurich to visit with our sisters for a week. I've asked Ruth if she can arrange for someone to meet me at Dulles at 3:15 p.m. Maybe Frank or Laurie can come—I know it's sort of out of the way and traffic coming home may be bad.

Lois, I'm glad to hear you're doing well! May it continue!

The rains have finally come to Mkar! Praise God! We are busy planting trees: one small maleana forest, one mango orchard, and two orange orchards. While the trees are young we'll farm in between the trees for the orchards – yams and cassava. We are after income generating projects!

I'll see you all soon!

Lots of love,
Florence

Letter Sixty-eight

116 Forest Avenue
Catonsville, MD 21228
24 July 2000

Dear Family and Friends,

Greetings once again, this time from the west side of the ocean! As I prepare to leave in just one more week, the time gets hectic as it always does. I want to say a mighty THANK YOU to everyone for the many, many thoughtful and generous things you have done. You certainly have made me feel very appreciated and supported in what I am doing in Africa. Know that I don't and can't do any work alone. God is there and each of you is really there through your love and support. Be assured of my prayers for you and the various and many good works that you are all involved in. I was reassured to hear how much goodness and good works abound here.

I promised many folks that I would include information about sending money to support the work in Africa. The safest way is to send a check to:

School Sisters of Notre Dame
4500 West Davis
P.O. Box 227275
Dallas TX 75222-7275

You need to include a note or something written on the memo line if you want it designated for the work in Africa. You might want to say:

– to support the sisters in the District of Africa or

– for the Project at Notre Dame, Mkar in Nigeria or

– for scholarships for the students at Notre Dame, Mkar in Nigeria.

If you say the District of Africa, it will go toward our general support – feeding, clothing, education of the young sisters, etc. If you specify where it is to be used, that will be honored.

One of the things that we have to do to become a Province is to become more financially independent. To this end we are in the process of setting up a Development Office for the District. It will be located in St. Louis at the Motherhouse and run by Sister Ruth Emke SSND. I want to send her a list of names of those who have been supporting our projects over the years through me. Hopefully, you might get a copy of our Newsletter as well as requests! To generate the lists, I've already asked some people to act as "captains" and help disperse this letter of mine to people who are in their same "circle." Erin Hayden will circulate the letter to the scripture group, Annette Duffy Heaps to INDians, Marta Johnson to former SSNDs, Sister Dorothy Hunt to SSNDs and my sisters to all others. If you don't want to be on such a list, just let me know! If there is anyone else who would like to get the letter, please feel free to circulate it yourself. If the person is willing to be on our Development Office list, let us know.

There were ever so many offers of helpful information or contacts that were given to me while I was here. I am so happy for these! I look forward to trying to dry tomatoes, construct that piggery and get some animals from the Heifer Project, etc. Any other ideas are most welcome!

Do you remember the parable of the elephants? The herd wanted to move on because the green grass was almost finished, when a young mother elephant delivered a new baby. The baby had a problem with the joints of its front legs and could not stand, though it kept trying repeatedly. If the baby or mother were left, they would be lunch for the wild lions. The herd was noisier each day as they tried to let it be known that it was time to push on to greener pastures, but they didn't want to lose that young healthy female – and she wouldn't leave her baby. In 3 or 4 days, the baby (probably too big for its mother's womb to develop the front legs properly) was able to walk, but slowly. The herd had no choice but to slow down. Somehow, I think that mother elephant is making herself known more and more! The developing world may be handicapped at the present time, but I do believe it is strong and healthy in many other ways that will be useful to the "herd' in future. Let's pray for patience, solidarity and compassion for everyone!

I also wish each one the special blessings of this Jubilee year. May the land of your own heart lie fallow so that the hand of the attentive Gardener may till and renew it. May we all have more listening and loving hearts that will allow our God to bring about the Jubilee justice so longed for by all of us!

At the end of this letter is a list of the books on Jubilee promised to those who made the retreat at the Oblate Sisters of Providence. I have only read the one by Harris, so if you read any and find it especially good, please let me know.

With love and prayers,
Gabriel

Proclaim Jubilee by Maria Harris

Three Mile an Hour God by Kosuke Koyama

Sabbath Time by Tilden Edwards

The Overworked American: The Unexpected Decline of Leisure by Juliet B. Schor

Keeping the Sabbath Wholly by Marva Dawn

Sabbatical Journey by Henri Nouwen

Jesus, Liberation and the Biblical Jesus by Sharon H Ringe

The Politics of Jesus by John Howard Yoder (Andre Trocme)

The Human Condition by Hannah Arendt

Learning to Forgive by Doris Donnelly

Children of War by Roger Rosenblatt

Love Beyond Measure by Mary Lou Kowacki OSB

Friends and Prophets by Elizabeth Johnson

These titles came from the footnotes of Maria Harris, and there are lots more. Happy reading!

Letter Sixty-nine

From: ssndmkar@infoweb.abs.net
To: lroeder@bwwonline.com
Sent: Thursday, August 03, 2000 6:38
Subject: Safe arrival

Dear Lois and Carolyn,

Hi! Greetings from the Infoweb Office on Victoria Island! The flight over was fine, thank God – a little late leaving each time, but no problems. Even the air conditioning was not too cold. Anebi's cousin was there to meet me in the Lagos Airport at the passport check-in and then helped me get my luggage on the trolley and past the customs check very quickly. I got to the MMM (Medical Missionaries of Mary) convent around 7 p.m. Tuesday and called Sister Anne's sister, Winifred. She came the following day around two p.m. That morning, I had already picked up the tickets from Ghana Airways, so I rested most of the afternoon.

There is an MMM sister who came in from Ireland yesterday who will carry my two big bags back to Ikot Ekpene. That is a big help! Coming back from Ghana I can now go directly to the local airport to catch a flight to Calabar or Port Harcourt. I will try to get a message to Peg to make arrangements to have the driver come down to meet me.

Many, many thanks, again, for all your wonderful help and support! I wish I could have given more in return. May God bless you with peace and health and joy in all that you do! Please relay the message of my safe arrival to others for me. Thanks!

With love and prayers,
Florence

Letter Seventy

4 August 2000

Dear Ange,

Greetings, dear friend! And how are you? I didn't get to call or write while you were in North Carolina. You were probably more than busy, but I wish I could have chatted with you one more time!

I pray Sheila and the twins are all well and doing fine. May you all enjoy these special days together! Thank God for family!

The last days before I left were a bit hectic. It seems no matter how I try to avoid that, I never do. I found out only Monday morning that my flight was confirmed all the way through, I was only able to get my thyroid medicine the day before, etc, etc. Lois and Carolyn were wonderful, as usual, helping out in whatever way they could. Ruth and Bernie had a farewell party Sunday night. Some of my Nigerian friends, whom I hadn't had a chance to see, were also invited, and we had a lovely evening. God is so good!

My journey back was fine. I am at the convent of the Medical Missionaries of Mary. I was able to change some money, pick up our tickets to Ghana, and send an email to Lois and Carolyn saying I had arrived safely. Today I'm relaxing, tomorrow we fly to Accra in Ghana for our 1st Education Conference. I hope to send a longer general letter soon. Know you are loved and appreciated, Ange!

Flo

Letter Seventy-one

21 August, 2000

Dear Family and Friends,

My greetings to everyone from Ikot Ekpene! I am still on my way back to Mkar, but getting closer and closer. The return trip was fine. Lois and Carolyn made sure I got off well from Dulles, and the rest was very smooth. I spent a few days in Mafoluku, Lagos with the MMM Sisters while I picked up our tickets for Ghana, made arrangements for Sharon to pick hers up somewhere and then called her in Jos. I thought I would sleep, but the place was noisy – Muslims in the morning, planes from the international airport during the day and the Charismatics at night. Ah, well!

Our Education Conference in Ghana was wonderful. It was our first for the District of Africa. We formulated an Education Mission Statement, for which I was very grateful. We still have lots of work in front of us as far as formulating policies is concerned, and this was a great start. I flew back with two of the Nigerian Sisters and LOTS of luggage, so we went straight to Port Harcourt from Lagos and got a taxi for Ikot Ekpene. I've been sorting out my homework and meeting/greeting people since then. On Wednesday, I will go back up to Mkar. Sister Inez will go along and continue on to Jos, and one of the affiliates will also come along to Mkar. Peg is due in on the same day from a bursars' meeting in Ghana, though she may not make it back to Mkar that same day. It will be good to get back. I pray I find everything green, since we are having good rains!

It looks like I will be staying in Jos for September, October and November. Sharon is due back from her surgery by then. Then I will return to Mkar while Peg gets her home leave in. When Carol Kleba takes her home leave sometime in the new year, I will go down to Akwa Ibom and stay with the postulants for three months. So, I will be a bit of a pilgrim it seems. However, I hope we will be able to get some building done in between! We received a $25,000 grant from the Propagation of the Faith for the construction of the convent at Mkar! Alleluia!! One more like that and we should be able to finish the convent!

There is someone going to the States on Wednesday, so I am trying to manage this electric typewriter to get off a short letter to let you know I have reached the continent safely. My address in Jos is P.O. Box 2274, Jos, Plateau State, Nigeria. Although I have homework to do in Jos, I hope I will have a bit more leisure. If so, I will certainly write again soon. My allergies are still alive and well, and I still need a sweater sometimes, even here! However, everyone tells me I look great (which means fat).

Many, many thanks to everyone for all the kindnesses throughout my stay in the States! I am really very, very grateful! Please keep us in your prayers often! And I promise to keep you in ours! May God bless you all with health and peace and joy.

With love and prayers,
Gabe

Letter Seventy-two

From: "SSND, Jos" <alnigeria@hisen.org
To: <lroeder@bwwonline.com>
Sent: Saturday, November 04, 2000 4:37
Subject: Greetings from Florence

Dear Lois and Carolyn,

Hi! I am still working at this email thing! We have just opened another address here in Jos. It is through Systems Link where we get our computers repaired. If you read this, be sure to let me know!

Tomorrow, Sunday, I will drive up to Kano with the driver to pick up two SSND visitors from Rome. They are coming for visitation which means they will go to every house and see every sister. They will leave Jos on Wednesday and I will meet up with them again in Makurdi when we gather for our Area Assembly.

My greetings to everyone!
Lots of love, Florence

Letter Seventy-three

From: "Sis. M. Gabriel Roeder SSND"
To: lroeder@bwwonline.com
Sent: Friday, December 15, 2000 12:36 PM
Subject: Christian Science Monitor

Dear Lois,

Greetings to you and Carolyn! I finally got my new hard drive installed! I picked it up in Otukpo on my way back up from Akwa Ibom to pick up the generator from Ikot Etuk Udo. Jos is the only house with no generator so we were unanimously selected to have it when we withdrew from there. The generator will help us with communications since we need electric power to send E-mail.

We are having a small generator house built and the machine is being serviced. We are also getting a IDD phone which should be installed any time now.

Both packs of the newspapers came – one to Mkar and one to Jos. Thanks so much! It's great of you to send them. On Wednesday I will be going back to Mkar. I will only come back up if there is something specific I have to do – which is likely, unfortunately. The bank accounts which had only Sharon's name are still not settled. Nothing is simple or quick here and certainly not routine! However, in general, I expect to be at Mkar until 9th February. We have an Area Assembly that weekend, after which I will go to Uyo to be with the postulants for a couple of months. Greetings to everyone! I will try to E-mail folks for Christmas, but I have to stop now to get ready to go for Mass.

Lots of love, Florence

Letter Seventy-four

From: "Sis. M. Gabriel Roeder SSND"
To: "Lois Marie Roeder" lroeder@bwwonline.com
Sent: Sunday, December 17, 2000 6:59 AM
Subject: E-mail addresses

Dear Lois and Carolyn,

Greetings from Jos! I am sitting here at my laptop trying to figure out how to use the address book. As I started to add addresses, I realized I don't have many with me. Maybe not everyone has email, but they most probably do. I have you and Laurie, Jim and Bobby and that is all. If you have a family list, could you try to email it to me? I thought I would try to send Christmas greetings from here before I leave on Wednesday.

The system I am linked up to is supposed to work from Makurdi also, but since I've never tried it I'm not sure if that includes Gboko. If it doesn't, I won't be using it too frequently, that's for sure!

I hope all is well there with everyone.

Greetings to all and lots of love!
Florence

Letter Seventy-five

From: Sis. M. Gabriel Roeder SSND
To: Bob and Ann Roeder, Lois Marie Roeder, Jim and Robin Roeder, Laurie Ellen Semon
Sent: Sunday, December 17, 2000 10:51 AM
Subject: Christmas Greetings

Greetings From Jos!

This seems like a wonderful opportunity to send you Christmas greetings! May your Christmas be blessed and joyous, and the New Year be filled with goodness, truth and beauty!

I pray all are well and enjoying the wonderful season of expectation! We are in the dry season here, with dry days and cold nights, longing for rains and greenery. It is a kind of winter for me. The poor and hungry that roam our streets and beg at every corner make me long for the Kingdom even more! The feeling of helplessness is keen, to say the least. God will do what we cannot.

Effort at eradicating the corruption continues, with a little progress now and then. The henchmen of Abacha are beginning to betray one another. We long for justice and peace and pray daily for our own conversion. May the Kingdom come soon!

The faith and jubilant life of the people are a constant source of hope that God is truly in our midst. Do remember us and pray for us.

With lots of love and prayer for you,
Florence

P.S. I have only four email addresses: Lois, Laurie, Bob Jr. and Jim. If anyone can help me out with others, I would be ever so grateful!

Letter Seventy-six

30 December 2000

Dear Ange,

Hi, dear friend! How are you? And all your beautiful family? I pray all is well and that you are able to enjoy one another!

I am back in Mkar, alone – but of course, never alone. Folks come by to greet, to lay out their troubles, or ask for advice or help. And in between, I am catching up on things – things for myself and things in the house. It is a lovely change!

Since I had a new hard drive put in the laptop, I was trying to send out Christmas greetings by email, though I didn't have as many addresses as I thought I did. Some came back because I made a typing mistake. I had typed a letter to you, but the printer wouldn't print. Yesterday I went to Makurdi to send the email, and I couldn't turn off the machine! I've removed the battery and will wait until I get back up to Jos to get the blessed thing fixed – AGAIN. When the computer works, it's wonderful, but when it doesn't, I waste time, money and energy galore!

I didn't finish what I tried to do in Jos – sort out Sharon's things. There are six bank accounts with only Sharon's name – student magazines, student societies, grants for the poor, for building. For us to have access to the money is a long process – going through the High Court. I'm still not finished, but I'm nearly finished. I'll go back up in a week or so. I did manage to get the used generator up to Jos from Akwa Ibom, sorted out estimates for a generator house and got that started, and got an I.D.D. phone line in – international direct dial. We can call and send faxes anywhere now – from Jos. Fax will need electricity, but the generator will soon be ready. Our inaccessibility communications wise is always a big problem. And Mkar is the worst of all the houses!

Here in Mkar I feel "wrapped around" with the poor. So many people are sick or need financial help. I listen and listen and listen! At least I can give my attention and concern. One of our younger watchnights (father of five) has a liver disease and looks like death. I'm told he can get better, but it will take long. Do pray for him – Emmanuel Tor.

If I can get hold of the word processor, I will be writing a general letter to send back with Fr. Dan Melaba. In the meantime, know you are much loved, Ange! I think of you often. Your loving friendship is a support and encouragement to me!

With love and prayers,
Gabe

Letter Seventy-seven

Notre Dame, Mkar
P.O. Box 501
Gboko Benue State, Nigeria
13 January 2001

Dear Family and Friends,

My greetings to you all! Belated greetings and my prayers

for God's blessings of peace, health and happiness in the New Year! My best wishes also for all the other occasions I have missed – Birthdays, Thanksgiving, Christmas, etc. I pray that everyone is well and happy and enjoying whatever is unfolding in your life.

Probably most of you know that S. Sharon Dei died unexpectedly on the 26th of September, 2000. That was very hard for all of us. I returned to Baltimore for the funeral, which was a blessing for me. Sister Grace Okon also went, the first time any of our Nigerian Sisters has been to the States. We stayed about 10 days. That was a wonderful opportunity for Grace and the Sisters of the Baltimore Province to get to know each other. My family and other Nigerian friends also helped to entertain Grace, for which I was most grateful!

When I returned here, there were remembrances and celebrations of Sharon's life here among us in Nigeria. This all helped us to accept and integrate the reality of her absence from our lives. There are still many things to remind me of her, but I thank God for her life and for all the good she did, especially here in Nigeria.

After I returned from Sharon's funeral, I stayed in Jos until close to Christmas. I sorted through her clothes, her file cabinet, her books, etc., and tried to put the bank accounts that had her name only in order. The latter proved to be a complicated process and is still not complete. I'm going back to Jos next week to try and finish it up.

While I was there, I did manage to get an IDD phone installed. This means we can call or fax anywhere from that line. I also got everything in place to build a small generator house for the secondhand Lister we received from the house we closed in Akwa Ibom. Maybe it will be functioning when I go back next week. This will give us "light" (electric power) to use computers and email which will also, hopefully, enhance the communication possibilities. The phone/fax number in Jos is 234(Nigeria)73(Jos)-610185.

When I went to Jos initially, to stay until Sharon returned, I took boxes of work for myself, thinking I would finally catch up with myself. I never even touched that! I brought it all back here to Mkar!

Just before Christmas we had two more funerals: the Bishop of Otukpo, 47 years old, and S. Chinyere Amadi's father, 90 years old. Funerals seems to be very frequent, aggravated, I suppose, by the poverty, lack of food and medication, stress, etc.

I spent Christmas here in Mkar by myself. The Nativity Sisters invited me for Christmas dinner, which was lovely. They are always very thoughtful and good to us. Throughout the week there were lots of folks coming to greet me and welcome me back from Jos. So the pace was leisurely and relaxed, for which I was very grateful. I enjoyed!

The dry season has its own unusual hazards here, abundant dust being the most obvious. The dust carries lots of germs and sickness. We have pneumonia, earaches, sore throats coughs, etc. One of our security men has a bad liver disease right now, probably from frequent malaria. He looks like an AIDS patient because he finds it so difficult to eat. We are helping as best we can, and the doctor assured us he is getting better, though it will take several months for him to heal.

Ants of every type imaginable come looking for water. You can find them on your sink, in the water filter, chopping roots of grass, bark of trees, etc. Our electric poles are just tree poles and every year we have to treat them with some poison at the base to keep the ants from destroying them. They get into ceiling boards, even facial boards and cause big trouble. We long for the spring rains, I assure you! At least I do!

In February I will be going down to Akwa Ibom for a couple of months to replace the Postulant Director. I can be reached there by email at ibbil@infoweb.abs.net.

We are expecting a grant for work on the convent and one for a piggery to help generate income for the school. For several months, cement has been scarce and expensive, but we are told that problem has been solved. I am hoping that cement will be plentiful by the time the money arrives!

Our school PTA is planning a launching on 12 May of this year for a school bus. It will also be an opportunity for an official "Opening" – a presentation of ourselves to some of the officials around. Do pray for us and for our work here. The school is doing well academically. There are problems which force us to reconsider having boarding, and we've not even finished building the school yet. We still need a dining area, an assembly area and a library.

My sincere thanks to all of you who have sent us help for the project here! It not only helps us and the students, it creates jobs for the people around when there is building – a life saver for many. May God bless you abundantly!

I hope to send this letter from Jos next week. May it reach you in good time! Take care of yourselves! I wish you God's blessing.

With love and prayers,
Gabe

Letter Seventy-eight

From: "debo debo"
To: lroeder@bwwonline.com
Sent: Monday, March 12, 2001 12:23 PM
Lois and Carolyn Roeder

Dear Family and Friends,

My greetings to each one! And my thanks for the many birthday greetings! It was a delightful surprise to hear from so many folks.

The little business is Gboko that now has email seems to work a bit. I sent a message up from here (Uyo) and it reached there. We also got one from Ghana. However, we were told that the address given to us was for the Company. We should be using: schoolsisters@yahoo.com.

We have received the piggery grant, for which we thank God. We are trying to make a shift in the estimate we submitted to allow us to use up the imperfect roof tiles that were rejected from use for the school and convent. We were also waiting in hopes that cement would be available to us at the depot, where it is much cheaper. Even as we wait, prices are going up. The value of the naira drops and drops! I wish I understood how that happens or who decides that it happens. It is surely killing us softly, as so many things do over here.

I never succeeded in finding out where to find anteaters, but now that the rains have started to come, maybe they will leave us alone.

The grant we received a year ago will probably reach us in a week or so; this one is for the convent. It can't finish it completely, but we hope to finish it enough to move in whatever part is finished. Someone asked how to send money safely. A cheque made out to School Sisters of Notre Dame and sent to Sister Ruth Hinderer at P. O. Box 227275 Dallas TX 75222-7275 with a note that it is for me or the Building Project at Mkar in Benue Nigeria will get it here. If you don't want to write a note, put my name or Mkar Bldg Project on the lower left line of your cheque. We are very grateful for all the help we can get!

Sister Virginia Brien is leaving us finally, to return to the States. She is 76 but still strong. I am on my way over to Ikot Ekpene to join in the send-off. It feels like the end of an era.

With love and prayers,
Gabe.

Letter Seventy-nine

Notre Dame, Mkar
P.O. Box 501
Gboko Benue State, Nigeria
28 May 2001

My Dear Family and Friends,

Greetings after a long silence on my part! I am sorry it has been so long since I have been able to sit down to chat with you at this computer. Email doesn't seem to be working around Gboko these days, and the post is so unreliable. Sometimes it is good, and sometimes – it is not good! However, I am finally back in Mkar, wearing my Building Director's hat. I do hope that everyone is well and happy, wherever you are, doing whatever you are doing.

I enjoyed my stay with the postulants in Akwa Ibom. I haven't had a chance to get to know these two young women much, so we enjoyed being together. It was also nice to teach again! The weather was very different, as was the daily routine and the surrounding language of the Ibibio people. There were many good folks and good things for us to enjoy together, and we did.

I returned to Mkar on the 10th of May – at the peak of the mango season, We are still eating giant, juicy, sweet mangoes. There are many varieties, but our favorite in this house is the "Peter". When they are ripe, you can bite off the tip and squeeze the juicy pulp through that opening. What a delight! It was great to get back home and settle into my old room and our own community routine. Sister Dorothy Enang will be leaving to begin her preparations for final vows, so by the end of this week we will be only three – Peg, Chinyere and I.

The graceful tree with the red-orange flower, the Flame of the Forest, was in bloom when I returned, as well as the bougainvillea and some other flowers. This, because of the fact that Benue had not gotten much rain yet. The Flame of the Forest is far more magnificent in Zaria, but it is still a pleasure to see it here.

One of the grants for the convent, given last July, finally came through in February, so I started moving on trying to plaster the convent. Cement is more expensive, and so are sand, labor and other things. The building world is altogether different from the time we first wrote for the grant, but we do what we can ! And we are grateful for every penny! I wish the grant could finish the convent, but it doesn't seem likely. Next time I write I will send some pictures of the convent.

Our masons and laborers are really so good, as are our regular workers. They are nice to work with. The day laborers are sieving plaster sand and stone dust. These are needed to plaster the walls and do the floors. Now that we have had a rain or two, the sharp sand is very decent. This makes the masons happy!

In addition to the convent, we are finishing off a large shed, which will house the block-building machine and the brick-making machine. The block-making machine had been under a shoddy-looking shed, in front of the new convent. This was near the front gate at the entrance to the compound, so you saw it as soon as you came in. It needed to be put somewhere, so we found a spot at the back of the school. That was built in January and it will probably take only a few days to finish it off.

We did receive the grant for the piggery. This project, by God's grace, will help us generate funds to subsidize the salaries of our staff. The area for the pig house has been cleared and the small building laid out. The excavation for the foundation was done on Saturday. Tomorrow the mason will blind that for building the German (concrete) floor. We are hoping to involve many of our staff in the running of this project. So far, we have had a seminar on pigs and piggeries for them, given by two vets from the State.

The two men talked about many interesting things, one of which was African swine fever. This wiped out a lot of the stock in this area a few years ago. Since people here like to eat pigs, they travel to the next state to buy them. So we are hopeful that we can take advantage of that situation to help ourselves. (We are still struggling because of the recent raising of the minimum wage; we've not been able to get the tuition up high enough to meet it!)

We were also able to send two staff to a one-week workshop on Monitoring and Evaluating the project, conducted by the grant givers. People here love such opportunities, and it stimulates their interest lots. The two staff will share their experiences with others soon, and then try to give the workshop themselves – that is their assignment! Now that there is activity on the ground, I hope interest will increase more.

One of our Nigerian sisters went to the Pan-African Conference on human trafficking held at Abuja earlier this year. Because SSND has NGO status with the U.N., we had an invitation. The sister who went, Regina Oluoh, was aware of the problem of many Nigerian girls being taken to Italy and other places in Europe before she went, but still found the presentations shocking. She has been trying to spread the word among the girls in secondary schools to warn them of the deceptions that lure them to such places. Poverty makes people so desperate; they grab at every straw! Most of the girls think they are going for jobs, – decent jobs. The wife of the Vice President and the wife of the Governor of Edo State are very interested and doing a lot to help in the rehabilitation of these girls. It is a dreadful problem, but at least it is out in the open, so many hands can help. Thanks be to God!

Added to that, we have just recently been made aware of the publicity given to the problem of sexual violations of indigenous sisters in Africa, mostly by indigenous priests. The many faithful religious found it very hard to listen to the broadcasting of this predicament, but want to take serious measures to help correct the situation. Please pray for the Church in Africa! This involves a problem of patriarchy, a problem of culture, and a problem in understanding religious commitment and priesthood. It is also aggravated by poverty!

I had a lovely, directed retreat at the Carmelite Monastery in Nsukka, Enugu State after I left the postulate in Akwa Ibom. I was able to savor a bit of Carmelite spirituality, and John of the Cross in particular. During the retreat I read some of John's poetry; now I'm reading a beautiful little book called The Impact of God by Iain Matthew. I recommend it highly! I never have enough time to read all I would like, unfortunately.

I hear a very gentle rain beginning. Much as we need rain for the farms, we had rain last weekend that drenched the plaster sand and stone dust so, that we were not able to sieve today. Looks like we won't sieve tomorrow either! We spent today planting maleana trees. (I only supervised.) These are hardy but commercially valuable trees. We are planting a little forest between the power house and the piggery. So far we have 50 or 60 planted. We lost some trees last dry season when kids from around this area set fire to the dry grass looking for field rats to eat. These are a great delicacy for them, as well as a source of income if sold. Especially at the end of the dry season, you will see kids along the road holding out their sticks with field rats neatly arranged, hanging from them.

I need to sign off so I can get this ready for Sister Betty Rosser who will be coming on her home leave to the States in June. Luckily, she is here doing some vocation work until Thursday, so I can give her this by hand to mail in the States. Betty had her 75th birthday this month! Amazing lady! !

You are all remembered often! Do take care and enjoy the lazy days of summer.

With love and prayers,
Gabe

Letter Eighty

Notre Dame, Mkar
P.O. Box 501
Gboko Benue State, Nigeria
24 June 2001

Dear Angie,

Greetings dear friend! How are you? I pray you and all those you love are well and happy – enjoying your growing family!

It has been long since I've heard from you, but the post here is so poor! You may not have gotten my last letter either. At any rate, I am fine. Hopefully, you have gotten my last general letter via Carolyn, so I won't repeat the contents of that here. The main reason that I am writing, is to let you know that some of the money you gave me while I was at home was given to Sister Peg, the principal of the school. You were very interested in helping someone with her tuition, and I have been meaning, for long, to let you know that was done. I am enclosing the picture of the girl who was helped. Her name is Hembadon Gesa, and she is in SS 1. That would be equivalent to sophomore class or grade 10.

The economic situation here continues to grow worse as food prices increase. We had the additional problem of a boundary war just a few kilometers from here. The tension was terrible, with many people fleeing their homes. Some houses were burned and farms were destroyed. Things have settled down now, and we thank God for peace each day. The war was between two clans of the same tribe! Over a relatively small piece of land, but the dispute is old!

I am busy, but more relaxed now that I do not have the leadership role with all the traveling and meetings that entails. With two constructions going on at the same time, I am busy – and challenged by the frustrations that go with it. Prices rise almost every day, so it is hard to plan well. The rains have interrupted the sieving of plaster sand and stone dust, which are needed for the plastering that is going on in the convent, but we do what we can. Lots of local boys are here every day looking for work to get school fees or meet other obligations, so there is no lack of labor!

This is planting season, so we are planting items that will be food for the pigs – whenever we get them! That includes cassava and soybeans. The pig house is almost finished, but we will have to put a gutter around it to protect the foundation from the water coming down the hill. Perhaps by the end of July it will be ready for occupancy. I pray God will bless that project! Its purpose is to provide extra income to supplement the salaries of the staff. You will surely be hearing whether it is successful or not!

May God bless you, Ange! You are often in my thoughts and in my heart, faithful friend! Please give my greeting to all those whom I know.

With love and prayers,
Gabe

Letter Eighty-one

Notre Dame, Mkar
P.O. Box 501 Gboko
Benue State, Nigeria
31 July 2001

Dear Family and Friends,

My greetings to each of you! And my thanks for notes, greetings, gifts and prayers! Even though channels of communications are sluggish over here, it is always good to know people are thinking of me, no matter how long the mail takes! Many thanks for trying and persevering. I pray everyone is well and happy, enjoying life as it has unfolded for you. Since this is July, almost August, many are no doubt on holiday. May you enjoy the lazy days of summer, and be refreshed at least by a different routine!

The rains have been coming rather slowly here in Benue State this year. The farmers are not happy because we haven't had a good rain for some time. The first harvest that rain brings is always the termites. When there is a serious rain, the termites come out in droves at night, gathering around our security lights. People come with buckets to sweep them up as they fall to the ground. That they provide good protein for the poor is their only redeeming quality! Otherwise they spoil houses, trees, plants, grass, etc. I was recently told that one of their natural predators is the scorpion, of which we have plenty. Still they survive! Not just here, but throughout the State.

Tomatoes are in and groundnuts, so folks are busy at the market. What is different this year is that the prices of food are so high. The economic picture here is always bad for the poor. In the big cities, people are building and buying, spending big, big bucks. Here in our little village people are hungry and can often not afford to go to the hospital when they are sick.

Our pig house is completed, at long last. It has 4 rooms in it. By God's grace, we will go to Jos this weekend to buy our first pigs. The project is meant to generate money to provide some income for the school to supplement the salaries of the staff, so please pray for its success. We will be getting 8-week-old weaners. We have planted soybeans, guinea corn and cassava for their food. The staff who so wish will participate In the running of the project, and the students who take Agri Science will also be involved. By the next lime I write I should have pig stories to tell!

We had a real scare a few months ago. Two of the Tiv clans were at war with each other over a piece of land. Where we live is inside the Ipav clan. Very close by, a couple of kilometres from the school, is the boundary with the Ukan clan and the disputed land. We were able to hear the gunshots and see the smoke where they burned houses and farms. The word was that the Ukan were out to destroy Mkar, especially the hospital and our school. The nervous tension was everywhere! I received a message to stop the work at the site because the Ipav did not want anyone from outside the area around. Some of our workers were from Gboko, and some of our laborers were Ukan! We stopped work and closed school, sending everyone home for a week. The Ukan who were living here fled, but some were killed, just because they were Ukan. Some had grown up here, so the situation was pathetic. We now have displaced persons whose houses were burned, people with families whose farms were uprooted and destroyed. They are desperate for work to get money to feed their children – and there is hardly any work to be found.

There is another skirmish in Latia, Nassarawa State, between Tiv and Hausa that has displaced many people and a third one in Taraba State, between Tiv and Jukon. Life was tough before all this started, but the fighting has made it a nightmare for the poor. Do pray for us!

We have finished plastering the new convent, thanks be to God, and we are now working on floors. The laundry and bathrooms have a simple red brick tile; most of the remaining floors are now being cemented. If money allows, we will put terrazzo or tile in the front part of the house where traffic is more. I hope to include a picture of the convent with this letter, though it was not plastered when we took the picture. Prices keep going up so it is hard to know how far money will reach!

Because people are so desperate for money, I have had an army of youth at the gate every day looking for work. I can't pay much for daily labor, but we have been able to get a lot of work done that wouldn't have been possible otherwise. We have cleared "bush" and planted some orange orchards, for one. Oranges seem to grow all year long here, and they are a great cash crop. We supply the north, where oranges can't grow, so they are always in demand. And the wonder of it is that orange trees can grow in stony ground. We are rich in stony ground! I'm told you must keep the grass cleared around the trees, and I know they can't survive fire. (People burn grass here at the end of the dry season, so that is always a danger.) Over the years, we have planted many trees, half of which have not survived. However, we now have over 100 orange trees! When they begin to bear fruit, this will also help to subsidize the school. We have a good number of palm oil trees growing (very slowly!), a few mango trees and several maleana trees. The latter can be sold for electric poles if they grow straight enough, otherwise they are at least good for firewood. We actually planted them for shade for the generator house, not for money!

Employing these mostly young fellows has been a conversation piece for us to say the least. Some need money for food, some are trying to get school fees, some need a pair of shoes or clothes. One was a refugee from Taraha State trying to get transport money to go back and look for his wife. They have done a mountain of work for us over the weeks, and been delighted to get their cash. Some who came were really children who could only cut grass or clear stones. These often gave their money to their parents, but some used it to "rent" a bicycle from another kid so they could learn how to ride! (We tried to know who the children were in case they were playing hooky!) They don't always know English very well, so there are days that I live and move in a tower of Babel, believe me!

We are getting, ready for an SSND African District Assembly that will be held in Makurdi in mid-August. Sisters will be coming from Kenya and Ghana to Lagos, then to Abuja where we will meet them. As of now, we have only gotten the flight information from half of them. We try to use email, but ...! Our getting together is always fun and work. There will be meetings, large group and small groups, minutes to take and type, frustrations that will come when the water or light fails. But one evening we will bring in our favorite dance troupe, the Ebony Dancers, who are terrific. They use beautiful traditional costumes, native instruments, of course, and do traditional dances from around the country (Nigeria). We always enjoy them immensely! There will also be a trip to Mkar so the sisters can see the school and the new convent. There, our students will do some cultural dances to welcome the visitors, and some of the parishioners will also be invited to come and help us welcome them.

Many thanks to my sisters and Dorothy Hunt who multiply this letter and send it around to family and friends for me! If you are able to share the picture of the convent, I am doubly grateful! May God bless us all as we try to enable those around us and build a world where all feel welcomed!

With love and prayers,
Gabriel

Letter Eighty-two

1 Sept. 2001

Dear Lois,

Hi! And thanks for your letter. I was so glad to hear some of the details of Margaret's death. She was really a great lady!

Louis was very, very kind to think of me with the generous gift in Margaret's name. The process used in sending the money was the best. It is quite safe. Our problem here in Mkar is that the "spreadsheets" with the information is slow coming—or does not come at all. The last sets were 3 months late. Peg, our bursar, was going crazy because she couldn't finish off the end-of-the-year (fiscal) accounts. She said the sheets must have been lost in cyberspace! Uyo and Jos both fare better than we do.

At any rate, I did get the information and I did write to Louis Hamilton. Hopefully by now he has received my letter of appreciation. Your letter arrived 30 August, less than 2 weeks after you wrote it.

None of our workers were killed in the war, Lois. Some ran for their lives, some had close calls, but no one died.

I'm delighted you are thinking of coming for a visit! I hope to come home in 2003, but no plans yet. Lots of love to you, Carolyn, et. al.

Florence

Letter Eighty-three

6 October 2001

Dear Lois and Carolyn,

My greetings to each of you from Mkar! I pray all continues to go well with you. You must surely be enjoying the transitions of autumn by now.

Sister Jane Weisgramm brought back lots of magazines covering the trauma of 11 September. I can imagine you have all been inundated with it. CNN was carrying it here, but we don't have T.V. The effects of the event, and reflection on it, must be heavy indeed over there. Everyone here just feels so bad—very sad and very vulnerable.

We received with delight Louis Hamilton's box of tools, which S. Betty carried back. I understand you provided the money for the overweight and also helped Betty out by running back for the small carry-on which came. You are so good! Thanks so much for all you did to help. I'm sure I don't even know it all. Betty gave me $100 + change from whatever you gave her.

Thanks, too, for getting copies of the picture of the convent around. I didn't realize that they would be so expensive. Carol Kleba had gotten a whole page of colored passport photos done—25 or so—at a very cheap rate, i.e. the same photo "multiplied" many times. Is that what you did? Does Kinko's do that? At any rate, I didn't mean to just drop that expense on you. I'm very grateful to you for taking care of it! The pigs continue to grow every day. A team from the group that gave the grant came last week and were full of praise for the project. We were really so happy! Now if they will just increase and multiply and generate income for us, all will be well!

I've been down a bit with a yeast infection in my intestines and another in my urinary track. Midway through the course of medicine for the second, they changed the medicine because the culture from my urine showed something was "gram-negative." After that I picked up much faster. I am still in medication for 2 more days. After that, I'm sure I'll feel more normal. My body has never been medicine-friendly!

I'm teaching 2 math classes this year to SSI—10th grade. It has been interesting being "inside" the school. Kids are still dribbling in, even as we enter the 4th week. The hardest part is getting to know the names of the girls, or even learning how to pronounce them.

We are expecting some more money for the convent in a week or two. I'd love to finish it before Christmas! Greetings to all! Take care of yourselves!

With love and prayers,
Florence

P.S. Please tell Joe we enjoy his scrabble game LOTS!

Letter Eighty-four

Cape Coast, Ghana
10 December 2001

Dear Family and Friends,

Greetings from Ghana! I hope all is well with each of you, and that you are enjoying good health and peace! This may or may not reach you before Christmas, but be assured of my good wishes for a blessed and joy-filled Christmas season! I also add birthday greetings for all those whom I have neglected, and good wishes for any other events that have been celebrated!

I came here to Ghana with several other SSNDs for a weeklong workshop given by S. Cathy Arata, our SHALOM coordinator in Rome. (SHALOM is our SSND network for Justice, Peace and the Integrity of Creation.) We met at Nsawam, where we have a convent and maternity clinic, and where our District headquarters is based. There is also a large Conference Center where we were accommodated. I have two days before my flight back to Lagos, so I came with a few others to Cape Coast to visit with an SSND friend, S. Mary Ann. Mary Ann is administrator of Mary Queen of Peace School here. This is comprised of nursery, primary and junior high – a "basic unit" school as it is organized in Ghana.

Let me start by expressing my own heartache over the catastrophe that took place on 11 September. At Mkar, we received the news a day or two after the event, but tried to follow the news as best we could. Peg was able to catch some footage of the actual event on CNN at someone's house, and I managed to plug in on the Prayer Service at the National Cathedral. Nevertheless, we were with you in mind and heart, praying for all of you, but most especially for those effected most directly by the bombings. As I read the news magazines, I can tell that the shock is still there. May God help us all as we struggle with the realities of our world!

Here in West Africa we are at the beginning of the dry season. We've not yet had a real harmattan, though it has been trying to come in. Schools are closing as the first term comes to an end. As you have probably read, in Nigeria as in many other places, we are having our share of conflicts. Most are tribal, over land, or political, interpreted as religious. We are not so near any of the conflicts as to be in danger, but we do see the "fallout" of the poor who are displaced. We have refugee camps in Makurdi, though most are now empty. In Mkar and Gboko, we have the poor who have tumbled onto the poor to find refuge. Food prices and medicine/hospital fees are high and sickness abounds, but everyone struggles on. We try to help as best we can.

I have a bit of news about myself. A few months ago I was asked to go to the Postulate at Mbribit Itam in Uyo, Akwa Ibom State to help with the teaching of the postulants. I have agreed to do that. I've been asked to try to finish the new convent at Mkar as soon as I can, and I'm trying to do that. At the moment, the "finishings" are in process – painting, louver windows, wardrobes, bathroom tiles, etc. My aim was that I would be finished at the end of December, but that might stretch into January a little bit. Our first Tiv and our first Igala women are among them; these tribes are from the Middle Belt – Benue State area.

The piggery is doing very well. Our four pigs, which share the common name of "Mbahiihii" are growing big and fat. The staff is organizing themselves to take care of the various aspects of tending to the pigs, and we are trying to do as much as possible ourselves. We grow the needed food, collected bones to grind for bone meal, mix their food, etc. The students are involved in some aspects in the Agric classes. At five months, the pigs were separated male from female. They will be mated soon – and then the fun will really begin! Little pigs take only 3 months plus to be born and they can come in big numbers. I am grateful to those who sent contributions to the project because we will probably have to expand the piggery very soon!

We are having major problems with the termites this year. They are always troublesome, but they have found their way into the rafters of our school, so our roof is endangered! Repairs will be costly, so pray for us! I wrote to the National Veterinary Research Institute in Vom (near Jos) in Plateau State begging for help in curtailing their destruction. Many people suffer from them here! If our scorpions are their natural predators, abundant as they are, I'd say the scorpions are losing the game!

My address at the postulate in Uyo will be P.O. Box 1903 Uyo, Akwa Ibom State, Nigeria. There is email address and a phone number, which I do not have with me here, but I will send along soon. We can never count on such things totally, but they have been good in Uyo for a while.

I have been trying to follow the news of what is happening in Afghanistan. As you may know, there was some reaction here to what happened on 11 September. Some Moslems are in sympathy with what was done, so they take out their resentment on Christians or foreigners. All this conflict seems to flow from the poverty and frustration that abound in this part of the world. We pray daily for the wisdom of our world leaders, that they may see with eyes of understanding and compassion, and find the way that will lead us all to peace and reconciliation!

Though I am due for home leave in 2002, I am not yet sure when I am coming. S, Carol Kleba, the postulants' directress is also going on home leave, so I need to work that out after I get to Uyo.

I'm on my way to meet Grade 6 for a while, so let me complete this letter before I go! I wish you all a Happy New Year with all the graces your hearts desire! May life unfold gently for you as we all move toward the future. I wish you God's blessings in abundance.

With love and prayers,
Gabe

Letter Eighty-five

11 February 2002

Dear Lois and Carolyn,

My greetings from Mbribit Itam! I hope you are both well and happy!

I arrived safely and was warmly welcomed by the Postulate community. I have settled in and begun teaching, though I am still organizing myself.

Your box of Christmas gifts arrived in Mkar before we left for our Area Meeting. What a wonderful surprise! Thank you so much for the thoughtful generosity! I shall enjoy each gift. The postulants are learning to do jigsaw puzzles, so I'll surely have company with that. And they love music! I am really very grateful for the gifts as well as the time and trouble to get them here.

Lois, I wish you a very happy and joy-filled birthday! I know you won't celebrate on Ash Wednesday, but you will surely celebrate 70 years. Can you believe we have come so far? Be assured of my love and prayers for God's blessings as the year unfolds. May it be special in all the ways your heart longs for!

Please send my greetings along to Joe. I assume he continues to be and do well. I missed sending him greetings, but I did remember him and Frankie in my prayers.

Greet the Schiaffinos and anyone else who would remember me. I hope to write a general letter soon. I'm almost finished writing the thank-you notes for all the "send-offs" from Mkar, so it will be coming soon.

I think I'll be coming on my leave 8 May for 3 months.

With love and prayers,
Florence

Letter Eighty-six

P.O. Box 1903 Uyo
Akwa Ibom, Nigeria
12 February 2002

Dear Family and Friends,

My greetings to you from Mbribit Itam in Uyo! I am happy to finally sit down and let you all know that I have arrived safely and settled in with lots of warm welcome! I have even started teaching and picking up a few other responsibilities in the running of the Formation House. So all is well with me!

I pray everyone is well there. For all those who had birthdays, Happy Birthday! Special Birthday Greetings to my sister Lois who, by my calculations, will be 70 Years old tomorrow. Can you believe we have come so far? It is a marvel! For all other celebrations – Valentines, Easter, anniversaries, etc., I wish each one many happy returns of the day!

Before I left Mkar, there were many "send-offs" held for me. The teaching staff did something, the non-teaching staff did something, and different friends did something. I am still writing thank-you notes! At the party from the non-teaching staff, with whom I worked most and whom I knew best, I was presented and dressed in "mure" cloth and given the title "Mure U Tiv", which means "Shade of the Tiv." I was very touched! I asked for someone to explain further what "mure" meant, which they did. I'll include the explanation with this letter so you can read it.

I was trying so hard to get everything finished in the new convent before I left, but it didn't work out that way. When I left the painter was still painting, the tile man was still working and workers were cleaning. I handed it all over to Peg, Inez and Chinyere. I was already a month late coming here. I talked to Peg on the phone today and it is still not finished!

The pigs have been mated, so everyone is counting the days until April. The staff is excited at the progress. Shortly before I left there was swine fever reported not far from us, so we were warning those who work closely with the pigs to be very cautious. The man from the Vet says ours is the best piggery in the State now, though probably the smallest! He included us in his report to the government in the hope that they might give us some assistance.

The last few weeks in Benue were really a surprise experience of harsh harmattan –"tropical winter!" It was so dry and so dusty. Peg and I both have curly hair under normal circumstances, but our hair was halfway to straight and sometimes had static electricity. Keeping the house free of dust was an impossibility, though we always tried. The insects and creatures that live in the soil become desperate, it seems, and come out looking for anything with a drop of moisture! The termites found their way to the wood in the roof of the school and the new convent, so we had an exterminator come in to fumigate. The problem of the termites led us to see other more serious problems in parts of the school roof – again. Some rafters were listing badly! The problem is from the contractor, however we have no choice but to correct it ourselves. The roof of the staff house and the convent are fine, thank God! The roof tile company did the staff house, and we did the convent by direct labor. Our carpenter had worked on the school roof and knew exactly what was needed.

Moving from Benue down to Nsukka for our Area Meeting was a relief for us from Mkar, but those from Akwa Ibom found the weather hot and dry! Life is so relative, isn't it? Now that I am in Akwa Ibom, my hair is as it was in the beginning, there is moisture in the air for skin and lungs, and we even had a rain last Sunday! But the harmattan came right back. Harsh harmattan means a better harvest when the rains come. We pray so!

Getting acquainted with my new community is most pleasant! And getting reacquainted with the food of this area is another enjoyable experience, especially the fruit that thrives here – banana, plantain, and pineapple. I shall miss the mango and year round oranges, but you can't have everything.

The class I am teaching at present (three times a week) is on Social Justice. I am learning lots as I go, and I am enjoying the course. I am supposed to be helping with music – singing and reading music (once a week), but each week something has pushed it aside. The five postulants are very good at singing and quick at learning new songs, so I think that class will be a joy, too. When Social Justice finishes (after about 12 classes), I will do Mariology. I did both of these last year when I was here substituting for the Postulants' Directress, so I am not overwhelmed with preparations. I read a bit the first time round.

Life in general moves forward slowly, seldom any rush. Only those who drive cars, motorcycles, etc. rush. Sometimes things work, sometimes they don't. NEPA (electricity) mostly does not work lately, or if it does it is half current – really quarter current! The phone works sometimes. The email company seems not to have noticed that mail is not actually going out or coming in. The road coming in to our place here in Mbribit Itam is in poor shape from last raining season, so when the rains come in earnest we will be in for great sport.

Some of that dilemma, I think, is part of growing pains. There are many more signs of people building new homes, or government building or renovating, putting in gutters, etc., which is an indication of growth or development. I think the electric (NEPA) and phone companies are working seriously to update, but are meeting major hurdles, though I am not sure. Just these last two days NEPA has been fairly good. There is great freedom in the press from what I observe, and people are eagerly reading newspapers and magazines a lot! And listening to the radio.

We do still have problems of fighting in different parts of the country, which is a great heartache to everyone. We are never sure what is behind them, and the situations are seldom treated in the news for fear of reprisals in other parts of the country. Please keep us in your prayers!

As it looks now, I will probably be coming for my home leave in early May for the usual three months. I'm still checking out things on my own schedule, and the cost and schedules of airlines. I look forward to seeing as many of you as I can!

Many, many thanks to all who have been sending letters, gifts, moneys for our projects, etc. I am really very, very grateful! Take care and have a Joy-filled Easter!

With love and prayers,
Gabe

THE TITLE: *MURE U TIV*

Mure in Tiv language means shade. This shade is presumed to come from a tree that has many leaves especially trees that are ever green. The article U in Tiv language means "of" so Mure U Tiv means the shade of the Tiv people.

As the geographical position of the Tiv people is in the tropics, and since the Tiv people are traditionally farmers, it is easy to understand that they value Mure (shade). The Tiv people believe that Mure is their only solace after being beaten by the merciless African sun in their farms.

As a consequence, your service in Tiv land is worthy of the title Mure U Tiv. For with your coming we have got a school of high standard which even our Federal Government could not have built for us. We wish to remind you that geographically, Mkar is placed exactly in the center of the Tiv people. As if the provision of the school was not enough, you have extended your services to touch individual lives. Those who were jobless, you have given them jobs. Those who were disabled in various ways, you have helped them beyond their wildest dreams. You have brought hope to the hopeless. You have brought help to the helpless just like the shade brings comfort to the Tiv farmer from the merciless African sun.

Perhaps we may not be able to list in this medium all that you have done for us, we wish that you may bear in mind that every iota of your service in this place is deeply appreciated and we pray that the almighty God who directed your steps to our fatherland should bless you as only God can give the blessings you deserve. We only hope that you will extend the same service to your new posting. Having known what service is, we also pray that you may involve us in your future plans so that we can borrow a leaf from you and serve other people the way you have served this place. Many thanks. May God Almighty bless you. Amen.

Letter Eighty-seven

November 26, 2002

Dear Carolyn,

Hi! And many thanks for your email. We do not go to Uyo to check for email every day, so that is why I do not respond quickly.

I did not receive anything from Lois. You said she sent me a map by surface mail. That one will take some time. I think you said the other was email. Whatever it was, I did not get that. Sorry! I'm sure you will let her know for me.

It was good to hear that Ann is doing well. I did send her a card. What of Alice O'D? And Louis H? Greet them all for me!

S. Carol Kleba, with whom I am working here at the Formation House, is leaving for a meeting in Ghana tomorrow. (She is different from the S. Carol Schmitz who has returned finally to the States.) She'll be gone about a week. She is a great organizer, so things will run easily in her absence. I'm teaching Sacraments, music, etiquette, Efik/printing, and typing 2. Can you imagine? The last three are just once a week; the others are three times a week. Actually, Sacraments is the hardest to prepare for because I've never taught them. And the subject is a very serious one for them. We don't have a textbook, so I have to prepare notes, type them, get them copied, put them together. I do it one sacrament at a time, so I can keep up.

We have eight postulants and they are from seven different tribes. Of the ones interested in coming next year, there are some from tribes I have never heard of. That is really a great blessing! At least, I think so. The youngest is 22 and there are two in their thirties. The senior postulants just went to Nsukka for a workshop in Journaling and loved it. For many, their experiences are very limited.

Our farm seems to be doing well. The fruit has appeared on the bean plants. We are getting "leaf" and paw paw and pineapple. I think the rains are almost finished. It is very, very humid. And the sun gets so hot!

I thought I would have done my "general letter" by now, but. The best laid plans of mice and men often go awry. Mine certainly do! Maybe by the weekend. I did want you to know that I got your email. Please give lots of love to yourself, Lois and all others.

Florence

Letter Eighty-eight

Mbribit Itam,
P.O. Box 1903, Uyo
Akwa Ibom State
28 November 2002

Dear Family and Friends,

My greetings to each of you! Today is Thanksgiving Day, so I know you are all celebrating together wherever you are. I pray it is a lovely day for everyone. The "terrorist tension" seems to have put a dark shadow on life from what I read in the news magazines. I hope it is not going to spoil this holiday for anyone.

I do hope you are all well and happy wherever you are, doing whatever you do! I am fine. We haven't had any rain for more than a week, so perhaps the harmattan has come. We had fog in the morning, and it has been a bit cool at night – sometimes. However, it is so humid during the day, it is hard for me to think of harmattan. In Benue, you had no doubt because of the dryness in the air. Here, it is impossible to keep dry. As soon as you start to do anything, any movement quickly brings the perspiration – and every layer of clothing is wet! The blah, gray sky of the harmattan is here sometimes, but doesn't last all day. And I've seen very few egrets, the lovely white bird that is also a sign of the harmattan.

We are all quite busy here at the Formation House, either teaching or studying. I enjoy the young women, and they seem to enjoy each other and enjoy being here. There are eight of them, and they are from seven different tribes: Igbo, Ibibio (2), Igara, Igala, Tiv, Mupon and Bette. They do not know each other's language, though they try to learn the greetings. They really have to communicate in English. Ibibio is the language of this area here at Mbribit Itam, so we encourage them to learn at least some of that language.

They range in age from 22 years to early/mid 30s. Some are trained teachers; some have secondary schools plus a diploma course in something like computer (probably without any "hands on" experience!). They are marvelous with music. They love to sing and play their native instruments to accompany it. They can harmonize as easily as I can breathe! And they learn new songs very quickly. I discovered that they like rounds, so they sing them any chance they get – when they are washing dishes, cleaning, for grace at meals, etc.

There are many things in the program for them to learn that are quite new experiences. They can now use a sewing machine and sew, they can type and will soon learn computer, they can crochet and embroider. The one postulant who had taken a course in sewing had never touched a sewing machine! In academics they are learning to outline what they read and draw time lines. They are being exposed to many new books and topics in theology, church history and spirituality.

We are already sorting out the women interested in coming next year. As one of our requirements we ask that they have 5 credits, that is, a "B", in 5 subjects in the exam that is taken to graduate from secondary school. This includes English, which many really struggle to get. So they re-sit the exam. That is an expensive proposition, so it is hard for them. Among those interested in coming, we also have new tribes represented: Esan, Kuteb, Tangale, and Ikwere. (The tribes we have at present among the professed sisters include Efik, Anang, Ibibio, Igbo, and Ngas.)

In addition to teaching and helping to run the house (some part of which is always in need of repair!), I keep an eye on our two laborers and the grounds. Our compound is probably about an acre, perhaps a little more. We have many plantain and banana trees, lots of luscious pineapples, and various beds of vegetables – tomatoes, vegetable leaf (from the fluted pumpkin), water leaf, ground nuts (peanuts), brown beans, melon and maize (corn). We took a risk with some of the veggies because this is a "second harvest," which means planting at the end of the raining season. Now that we have a borehole, we are hoping that we can manage if we need to water, which we are already doing. So far so good. The trees that I mentioned are fine. We also have orange, lemon, grapefruit and avocado pear trees, which are not doing well. We will keep working on it!

In addition to the farm products, we have many lovely flowers here – bougainvillea, pride of Barbados, mimosa (with no fragrance), red, whites and salmon hibiscus and others whose names I don't know. As you can imagine, we have various birds around as well, – some quite talkative.

Because what grows here, really grows, when the workers cut the grass, they shave some areas so that they are bald! I can't say I blame them. We cut grass here by hand with a cutlass, so it is backbreaking. I am trying to find some ground cover from among the various grasses to help prevent the constant erosion in some places. I believe there are as many wild grasses as there are languages! God's imagination is mindboggling, isn't it?!

Poverty and corruption are ever with us here, as are the riots that break out. We pray for peace every day! And we do what we can for the poor. The postulants go once a week to the women's prison (where they teach embroidery to the inmates), and the Remand Home, which is the children's prison (where they teach the 3 Rs). They do what they can to give the people whose lives they touch some sense of dignity through their care and concern. They have tried to get help or intervention for very sad cases, but seldom succeed. We are still trying to assist Elizabeth Sampson, a woman with epilepsy who has been cast off by her family. By now she must be somewhere between 35 and 40 years old. Of late she has been sleeping on the streets, which is quite dangerous for her. We do what we can to cajole the welfare system to assist, but it accomplishes so little!

5 December

I heard just today that a priest died in the riot in Kaduna. He was an older man, and he was terribly "hacked" all over his body. He lived a short while, but has died. May God help our pitiful world!

The last I heard, the pigs were doing well. Gift money enabled us to connect water directly to the pig house, which was a tremendous blessing. It is still a struggle to get enough food to feed them, and those who care for them say they need more space. Christmas is a big time for buying meat, so maybe more pigs will be sold. That would mean less to feed and less need of space! Many, many thanks to all those who helped us out on that project!

Sister Carol Schmitz has gone home for good. Peg Malone and Inez Bocklage are in the States for home leave. Second year postulants go home for Christmas, so our number is lean for celebrations! May your own celebrations for Christmas be blessed with joy and goodness!

With love and prayers,
Gabe

Letter Eighty-nine

22 December 2002

Dear Ange,

Greetings, dear friend! I pray all continues to go well with you. I received your 2 lovely cards/letters with great delight—it is always so good to hear from you!

I loved your beautiful butterfly! Aren't people so creative? It was so lovely that I will find a way to use it again! Your news of retirement and your elation was good news indeed! I am really so, so happy for you! You persevered so faithfully and so steadily at that job! And now is your time to relax and enjoy!

What a lovely mom and grandmom you are, Ange! And it is just like you to make your services into something you enjoy! I can almost imagine I am walking around the Harbor with you, enjoying the beauty, the bookstores, the treat of coffee and sweets! We really did enjoy such lovely times together! I too remember them with joy.

Your trip to visit Sheila sounds like a real adventure! I wonder how Sheila manages when she is alone?! You and Colleen were so good to invest yourselves that way—to share Sheila's time without Russell, sharing a "slice of life" with her.

Your second card was marvelous! The words were so perfect, so special! I wish you the very same greeting—thoughts of gratitude as many as the stars and reaching just as far! I hope your Christmas and New Year are filled with the blessings of love and peace and joy. I know your family will wrap you round with all of that! God made life to be such a gift! And I do pray for Michael. I hope he is following his star. Do wish Mike a happy, (belated) birthday for me!

I do hope our group gets together in January. There is something very special that happens in such "circles of friends." It must be a reflection of the Trinity, the first dynamic of love shared. I look forward to hearing how it all unfolds when you gather again!

Work here is getting to be a bit more familiar. Parts of it, I feel I am not good at, but we are just so short of "senior" SSNDs. In another 5 years or so, the indigenous sisters will be ready to take over leadership, I think. Part of my anxiety—and this is just for you, please—is that the Postulant Director is going home in February. I am the one to pick up her work. Another expatriate will come to stay and help, but with no formation experience. The Director, Carol K., seems burnt out, but she is a rigid person anyway. Trying to help her get through the remaining two months and also help the postulants, who find her hard, and help myself—is a balancing act to say the least. In some ways it will be a relief when she goes, but in others, I panic. She is bright, quick, a good organizer, handy with many things like cooking, sewing, typing, computer. Organizing the two year program frightens me. However, the one coming is a good organizer, so perhaps God is in control – oh, me of little faith!

One of the things that is uncomfortable here is the amount of physical work. We have a driver and 2 laborers who keep the grounds in order and double as watch nights—but no help inside this big house. I would love to have a woman come in to cook the noon meal and help with laundry and some cleaning. It would remove a lot of pressure from everyone. Carol has been adamant that the postulants do all the work, but some doesn't get done well under this system. I'm biding my time till she leaves—and hoping there is enough money to pay another employee.

At this moment, I am Director of Temporary Professed (3), covering for the Affiliate Director who is on sick leave – and so organizing a retreat for 14 women on 28 December, and assistant to the Postulant Director and conscious I will be carrying out her work in another 2 months. I'm not complaining, but I am distracted to say the least. Please, Ange, don't let any of this slip to anyone else.

The young women are very interesting. And Carol is very good and very objective in evaluating them! One was just asked to leave last week, so there are seven, from six different tribes. They all do well together, I must say. You would enjoy them, Ange! So many things are new to them—and they love learning new things—games, typing, crocheting, embroidering, making peanut butter, one another's language or recipes, printing, all the content classes—mostly theology—even etiquette! Though a couple of them still spit out their orange seeds or fish bones!

They are all attractive, bright women—good dressers, wonderful at music: singing, dancing, playing instruments, friendly, and so eager to serve God by serving others. All Africans seem to be so profoundly religious! They love to pray, to sing and dance for God, to fast, process, go to Church—but they love miracles and want God to make them rich and get rid of their enemies. Skin deep religion? Who knows?! We work to tame that without doing violence to their culture. Quiet prayer, self-knowledge and such are tough challenges for some of them.

Carol is herself a homebody, so the postulants don't go out much. They visit the VVF hospital next door and teach at the children's prison—and they shop. For me, that is a bit confined. Hopefully, I can ease that a bit. We have new leadership coming in next August. Until then, I can't know my future very clearly. My task until then is to help hold everything together. May God help me and make up for my deficiencies!

Ange, I am wishing you Happy Christmas and a Blessed New Year on this quiet, hot, harmattan Sunday in Nigeria! I love you, dear friend!

Gabe

Letter Ninety

Tuesday, February 25, 2003

Dear Lois,

Greetings from Mbribit Itam! And thanks for your email. I am so sorry to hear about Ann. I know she was suffering a lot, so it is a blessing that she has died. And that she died so peacefully is another beautiful blessing. I certainly did not expect that she would be gone before I return for my next home visit! You have been giving so much of yourself to her, that her absence must leave a big hole in your life! I can imagine you are behind in your agenda.

Actually, just after I sent my last email to Carolyn, I got hers saying that Ann had died. I'm not sure why our email is so fluky at this end! It really is frustrating. Anyway, I was glad to hear all about Ann's last days and her funeral. May she rest in perfect peace!

And I finally did get your two maps! And the booklets! Alleluia! They are really lovely! A great addition for us! Thank you so much!

I have really been hopping these past days. Sister Carol Kleba, the Director of the Postulants, has returned home for R & R. She has complained for some time now of excessive tiredness. She did not want anyone to know until the last gong, so I honored that. But I needed to learn everything about everything before she left. It looks overwhelming sometimes, so I just take it one day at a time. I hired a cook straight away to help with the midday meal

We are all praying for peace – peace all over this world! I want to pray that Bush will slip on a banana peel and crack his head. However, that would put Cheney on top, which would probably be worse! I did add my name to some list that came around on the email circuit. I got a response from the White House, saying they had received it.

Take care, Lois! Greetings to everyone.

Lots of love,
Florence

Letter Ninety-one

28 March 2003

Dear Family and Friends,

Greetings to each one after a long time! I have been hearing about the unusual heavy snows from everyone – along with other pieces of news, of course. I pray everyone is "out from under" all the snow and enjoying signs of spring by this time!

I have to tell you, we feel jealous of your snow. We are having hot and humid saunas here. And since the rains are coming, things are growing as if we were one mighty big hot house. We have flowers galore! – though many are children of the dry season.

I send my warmest thanks to everyone for all the birthday greetings and gifts which came, many through Peg and Betty. And my sincere thanks, too, for all the financial contributions! Many have come through Louis Hamilton. I hope to write to all those folks, but the spreadsheet that came is not clear about some of the monies that came. In time, I will catch up! We have had problems with email, telephone, regular post, etc., etc., etc.

I guess everyone knows by now that our Postulant Director went home for a much needed rest, so I am sailing this Postulancy boat into port. Sister Peg is here with me as part of the community and to do some teaching, and Sister Betty comes every week from Ikot Ekpene for two days to teach. I am doing my best to keep up with my own teaching and the various responsibilities and activities. No small task for my aging mind! The 1st year postulants are getting ready to go for their first home visit in a few weeks, and then move out for their apostolic ministries. The second year postulants are getting ready for a communications workshop, their first directed retreat (in Benin City) and preparing to leave for their novitiate in Ghana. Everything about those activities requires inquiries and more inquiries and planning, etc. If one of the postulants ends up in the wrong country at the wrong time, I will be to blame!

While Betty was in the States, I was covering her work, so it is wonderful to have her back. My work with the temporary professed is not a lot, but it does take time. After our elections for District Leader in April, there will probably be a formal appointment of a Postulant Director. It could be me, or it could be someone else. If I am the one, I think the position of Temporary Professed Director will be given to someone else.

Sister Peg is teaching computer to the postulants. Keeping such things in working order here could be a full time ministry. Only one battery backup is out of commission at the moment, so we are doing fairly well. The second year postulants are learning to use the mouse by playing solitaire and minesweeper – and loving it. They did typing last year, so they know all their keys. Sister Betty is teaching Heritage and Arts and Crafts, both of which are very popular with the postulants. My own portion is Morality, Community, and some music. I also meet with each woman for an interview every week. Then there is overseeing it all, taking care of the workers, etc. However, we are moving ahead smoothly, thank God!

One of my hobbies (distractions?) is tending some of the flowers. I am also directing the workers to control erosion and termite problems, trim and plant and weed and mend. The compound is fairly big – more than an acre, I'm sure. I am still testing out ground covers. One has been a great success along the north side of the house, where the rains carry sand down the slopped drive. It doesn't need cutting, – only some weeding of the tall grasses that appear in it now and again. The workers like this a lot! They want to plant it everywhere. The problem is that it dies in the dry season without water. And we don't have enough to put it everywhere. There is another "crab grass" in the front of the house that doesn't need cutting, so we are trying to make better use of it.

The best-looking grass that is lovely and green all year is a pain to cut (they cut grass by hand with a cutlass here). I do enjoy being "out of doors" because this work keeps me inside so much – in the office or in the classroom.

The workers are busy weeding and cutting grass. They have also planted more plantain trees and are now planting corn and melon (source of a seed used in cooking one of the favorite "soups"). When the postulants are cooking, they walk out into the garden and pluck leaves from one plant or bush or other. There are not so many vegetables here as we have in the States, though many have been introduced. However, the variety of leaves, and the knowledge of which ones are for what thing, is tremendous. There also seems to be a greater variety of beans and recipes for using them.

We are all praying every day for peace – here in Nigeria as well as in Iraq and the rest of the world. Our elections are coming up on Easter weekend. It seems like everyone is just hell-bent on winning that election! And there are strikes everywhere. I hope you are praying for us, too. We surely cannot bring order out the chaos – only God can.

There is still a steady show of construction going on one place or another. It is a sign of development, I guess – certainly a sign that some folks have some money! There are more "permanent" houses down in this area than in Mkar area. Now that Nigeria produces aluminum sheeting for roofs, they make colored aluminum sheeting – blue, green, gray, and a brick red. Sometimes you will see the roof in one color and the siding that seals the roof in another color. One roof not far from here has "stripes" of all these colors! And we continue to see more and more petrol stations being built, even though we can hardly find petrol at the moment! The stations are usually very attractive and rather elaborate. Often, I've thought a house was going up, only to see it turn into a gas station. I wonder if the maintenance problems in these new houses are like ours.

Thing are constantly "not working" or "spoiling." And if you send to the market to get a nut or a small part, you have to buy the entire fixture just to get your nut. Maybe it's like that over there as well?

Our postulants are really bringing such a rich cultural experience to our community life! They are learning each other's greetings and songs. At Mass we often have the Lord Have Mercy or the Lamb of God in one of their languages. Some of the postulants are from polygamous marriages, with many brothers and sisters. One has 30 brothers and sisters and 70+ some nieces and nephews–thus far! Her father had eight wives; six are still living. She insists that she knows all of these folks by name! Their adjustment to the culture of religious life "no be small!"

The postulants are all very interested in trying out native herbal medicines. We have a small book put out by the Benedictines here with many "recipes." One postulant used the leaves from a common eucalyptus tree ("thunder protector") to cure a recurrence of typhoid. Another combined bitter leaf and the yellow (old) leaf from the pawpaw tree for malaria with success. We may put all those pharmaceutical companies out of business! Unfortunately, all these herbal medicines taste bad!

I will be going to Ghana this year in mid-July for about a month. I accompany the postulants who are going to the novitiate. We have a Transition Program there for the women from the various countries to enable them to get to know each other and become a little familiar with their new surroundings. This year we will have women from Kenya, Nigeria and the Gambia. We are hoping for a new sister to come from Milwaukee around August, so perhaps I will be able to meet her on my return trip and accompany her back to Akwa Ibom. Her name is Sister Sandra Weinke.

At a point I had wonderful intentions of keeping up with personal correspondence, but I have failed again! Let me close this general letter with wishes for many blessings of health and peace and joy for everyone! Be assured that I am alive and well. You are in my heart and in my prayers!

With love and prayers,
Gabe (Florence)

Letter Ninety-two

22 July 2003

Dear Ange,

Warm and loving greetings from Ghana! I pray each one in your beautiful family is well and happy – especially YOU!

I am here in Sunyani, Ghana for a month. We are in south-central Ghana. We have some rain, though not at all like Ikwa Ibom. It is cooler, dryer and mostly overcast – so different. Those from Kenya are feeling hot, while the Gambians and those of us from Nigeria are chilly!

There are 10 young women from 9 different tribes coming together as a group and getting to know each other – as well as each other's cultures. The "feeling" here in Ghana is one of calm – gentle, relaxed people. However, the population isn't even one fifth that of Nigeria! No wonder many Nigerians are seen as aggressive – struggling for land, water, jobs, food, admission to school. Nevertheless, the experience of the program is rich, indeed!

Ange, thank you so much for your very generous gift. We pooled it with others and were able to buy a photocopy machine. I am ever so grateful!! It is really very, very helpful to us.

It is a bit of a relief to be here, finally. The responsibilities are far fewer. I feel like I move in circles each day, trying to get things to happen, get them finished, get something fixed – and at the end of the day it feels like I've accomplished nothing. The next day seems much the same! Hopefully, next year will be easier, though we will have new people around. The Postulants' Director will be new, we will have a new sister coming who will help with the teaching, and, of course, a new group of young women, four or five. The three first year postulants became second year postulants, so in all, we will be 9 or 10 in the community. Did you know Kathleen Feeley is coming to Ghana? – to teach in the new Catholic University starting here in Sunyani. (No buildings! They are using the Pastoral Centre!)

Much, much love to you, my beautiful friend! May God continue to shine through you!

Gabe

Letter Ninety-three

18 September 2003

Dear Family and Friends,

My greetings to each of you! I pray you are well and happy doing whatever you are doing! Time always seems to fly by here, and I foolishly wait for a lull, which never comes. We are just at the peak, or maybe slightly over the peak, of the rains here. We have had plenty of rain! It is probably not the heaviest raining season we have ever had, but it seems bad because the roads are so very bad this year. It can rain all day and all night! Some days you have to drive in water more than on dry land – the water being in big, sharp-edged potholes! It does a terrible job on our cars, as you can imagine.

From mid-July to mid-August, I was in Ghana with our four Nigerian postulants, as I mentioned I would be in my last letter.

They were in a Transition Programme; the directors were a kind of background support. There were four Nigerians, one Gambian and five Kenyans. Ten women from 9 different tribes! The dynamic among them was really beautiful to watch as they strived to get to know the folks from the other countries. They shared information about their cultures and listened to lectures on how to understand and get along with people from other cultures. They learned a lot and shared a lot. The music, song and dance of the different tribes were a wonderful treat for all of us. It was reflected in liturgies, prayer, and recreation. And all of this in a beautiful and relaxed setting! So I really enjoyed the month. Our four Nigerian postulants are now happy novices: Mabel, Mayi-ojo, Oyin-oza and Clara.

Coming back home was a shift in gears – from first to fifth. Inez and I met S. Sandra Ann and S. Mary Martin at the airport in Lagos. Inez had another meeting in Kenya, so she stayed in Lagos, but Sandy, Martin and I continued on the next morning to Calabar and then to Uyo. We were welcomed by S. Betty, S. Nentaweh, the three first year postulants and two volunteers from Germany! It was so nice that the house was open and functioning – even though the computer was deathly sick with a virus. We had many nice times as we all cleaned house and prepared for a celebration of thanksgiving for S. Ebele's profession. More cross-cultural sharing!

We are waiting for S. Marie Antoinette, our new Postulant Director, to arrive. She needs a paper from Immigration in Abuja before she can get her visa. (A new wrinkle for us!) Sandy and Martin also need that, but there was a mistake in the designated "category" on their visas. I have been trying to get this sorted out so I would only have to go to Abuja once, but that hasn't worked. I have been driving back and forth across town in all the swollen potholes (I drove into a gutter twice, not recognizing that the water and "stuff" I was seeing was not solid land). As of yesterday, I have sent all the documents up to Makurdi to a priest who has offered to help us out.

In this interim, we are trying to keep up with cleaning, cooking, laundry and living in this big house. The postulants are three in number and the rooms are 23 not counting toilets and baths! So we try, and do what we can do. S. Sandy began her teaching this week, creatively combining journaling with art, penmanship and heritage – Augustine and his journaling in the Confessions. We also have someone coming in to teach sewing now. Betty will come next week and do more on heritage – Alix le Clerc. I'm doing music, weekly interviews and the general overseeing of life.

These 1st year postulants made their first directed retreat and really loved it. It was just 5 days, but a totally new experience for them. They appreciated the silence very much.

It is always a surprise to learn the many experiences these women have not yet had. I bought a toaster with some gift money, and found that none of them had ever eaten toast or had any idea how the toaster worked. But they like it just fine! They get to like peanut butter quickly, and are adept now at many table games – Yatzee, Skippo, Monopoly, Chinese checkers, etc. Often their vocabulary is very limited, even though they speak English well with what they know. We have table reading at breakfast, just to keep ourselves aware of what they know and what they don't with respect to vocabulary.

We are having new spurts of armed robbery in our neighborhood. Thieves came to the VVF Hospital next door (on our left) on Monday night, and a small cooperative bakery, just down the road a piece, on Tuesday night. A couple of weeks ago, they visited our neighbors on the other side (right) plus a small hotel across the way. We are holding our breath and praying furiously. Insane as it sounds, this happens every year. Word is that the thieves are getting ready for Christmas!

I am very, very grateful to each of you for the donations sent over. We now have a 2nd computer, a 2nd hand photocopier, the toaster and we did some outside painting of the house. There are always such things to keep up with. Our challenge is the harsh weather – very humid, very wet, very hot. Machines do not like it at all. Actually, our bodies don't really like it either, but we can handle weather better than a machine.

Cybercafes are opening up more and more. Since our 2 phones still do not work (a year and a half now!) we use the cafes for email. There are many places from which we can phone, but it is a bit expensive. Some people want us to get a cell phone, but I see that as another machine that will probably not work and need fixing. I'm up to my eyeballs with that routine! I can hardly think of adding another. However, we may be forced to it soon.

Construction continues around us. Uyo, which is a state capital, is getting more "upstairs" buildings – some three and four stories. Some were started years ago, but stopped after the ground floor – and managed with that. Now they are being completed. A few are impressively modem. Signboards for stores are being renovated and look more colorful and professional. Even villages are putting signboards on the roads to let you know they are there – or just inside the bush a bit! If only we had a drainage system that could handle the tropical rains! Our roads would have a better chance of survival! I can imagine that will be terribly expensive.

You are all in my heart and in my prayers, especially Griffin and Bob and Ann with their "instant family."

Love,
Gabriel

Letter Ninety-four

From: Carol Kleba
To: Lois Roeder
Subject: Re: Sister Gabriel
Date: Wed, 31 Mar 2004 01:39:23 -0800 (PST)

Dear Lois,

I am Sister Marie Antoinette, the Postulant Director living with Gabriel at Mbribit Itam in Uyo, Nigeria. I tried to write you earlier, but my email was returned. I looked up some old emails and found that I did not have the 7 in the address.

Gabe wanted me to inform you that she has a lapsed, slipped disc and in on complete bedrest at present. Towards the end of February, Gabe was bothered by her sciatica and went to the doctor. He asked her to get an x-ray which she did. He confirmed that the sciatic nerve was the problem. He then recommended that she go to a therapist to help her with it. Gabe also did that. But early March, she got such severe pain that she could not walk. So she was put to bed rest, traction for the first five days and medication to help her muscles relax. Gabriel has had the assistance of two medical doctors in addition to the therapist. They all recommended complete bed rest with exercises to help the slipped disc to return to its rightful position.

I am sorry that my first email did not reach you. I hope that this one is successful. Gabe asked if you would inform the rest of the family for her. Thank you.

S. Antoinette

Letter Ninety-five

P.O. Box 1903 Uyo Akwa Ibom State Nigeria
15 June 2004

Dear Family and Friends,

My greetings to everyone! I pray this letter finds each of you well and happy! I also extend my thanks for the many "Get Well" cards and encouraging notes! I am very grateful.

Would you believe I am finally getting to complete this letter/email? So much time has passed I don't know how to begin! Prior to this episode with my back, life was fine, busy and enjoyable. S. Antoinette, our new Postulant Director, jumped in and made herself at home right from her arrival - that was back in October! Our postulants are a lovely group of women of very diverse backgrounds. We do enjoy getting to know them! Bette, Ibibio, Mupun, Oshibori, Tangali, Igbo, Kuteb and Tiv. Sisters Betty and Sandy came in once a week to do some teaching, and it was always a nice opportunity to be with them. Sandy has just come to Nigeria after teaching 20+ years at our Mt. Mary College in Milwaukee, so this is her "retirement." She and I studied at St. John's in Collegeville for six summers together, way back when! So we had a very busy and very pleasant year, enjoying the weeks as they flew by.

I was supposed to be teaching, but that got harder and harder with the various things that fell under my umbrella of maintenance - so I taught less and less as the year progressed. Our farm is doing fairly well, though we had to have someone come in to treat the soil against the kingdoms of ants that live beneath us. They chop the roots of various and sundry plants when they are thirsty, especially in the dry season. They are often in the house as well. We continued the painting on the outside of the house, as we were able to afford it. We also did a bit of work on the entrance drive, to counteract the erosion that had taken place. We added soil and stones and planted more hedge at the edges of the road. Our hedge has red flowers - it is very lovely. And, of course, there was always the daily liturgy of repairing whatever breaks or wears out. So, we were alive and well!

Elizabeth Sampson, a woman in her early or mid-30s who is an epileptic, has been living on the streets in Ikot Ekpene for some time. We have known her for long and have been helping her with medication and whatever else she needs. During the last harmattan we had a really cold spell, which left her unable to walk. We brought her here to stay at Mbribit Itam while we tried to get her some medical assistance. She has been sleeping in one of our garages since. She has rallied to the care and is doing very well, but she is still with us. In spite of much "running around" we cannot find any government or private agency that will take care of her, and she can't take care of herself. Please pray we find a suitable place for her.

Although I drove around the town a lot, I didn't travel long distances very much this past year. A relief for me! We had an Assembly in Mkar and I did go to a meeting in Kaduna in January. I took a night bus, not my favorite way to travel, but it is cooler. When I was in Zaria, Kaduna was a very familiar place for me, so I enjoyed meeting some old friends there. The meeting I attended was that of the National Conference of Women Religious, and I was the representative for Nigeria SSND. I always liked these meetings because the scope is that of the Church throughout Nigeria. One of the weighty items on the agenda was the focus of the new standing committee, COSUDOW, Committee of Sisters for the Dignity of Women. The Conference of Catholic Sisters in Nigeria supports an Office in Benin City to deal with the human trafficking problem. Most of the girls/women in Italy and elsewhere that are being trafficked from Nigeria come from around Benin City. The Sisters of the Sacred Heart, an indigenous community based near Benin, staff the Office. The Sister in charge, Sister Florence, is a lawyer by profession, and she has been very active, both in going to court, and in trying to get the women reunited with their families or rehabilitated through training/school. She is now trying to get an additional site in Ikeja (Lagos), near the airport, so she can have a place for the girls to stay when they are flown back from Europe. Our problem, of course, is always money.

Around the beginning of this year, I began to have serious problems with what I thought was sciatica. In March, I found a physical therapist - the only one in Uyo - who began treating me. After two weeks, following a ride to our convent in Urua Edet Obo - the road to which was particularly bad at the time, I had really bad pain in my back and collapsed when my left leg seemed to have a "black out." That was the beginning of my latest saga! I had a slipped disc, which required that I be in bed. I also had a problem with my sacroiliac. The sacrum kept slipping out of place. For more than a month, I was in bed. My paralyzed leg didn't gain much with the inactivity, as I am finding out now, trying to make the muscles work again! Since I couldn't stand or walk, I had to have everything done for me. Everything! But my community was wonderful. There isn't anything they didn't do for me! And they did it all gladly and graciously. I will be ever grateful.

Eventually I graduated to standing and hobbling, so I could wash myself and ease myself. Then I asked to go downstairs to the guest room, where all this was easier and I could get myself to the dining room with the aid of a walker. From there I moved to a stick, and now I am managing on my own. I have moved back to my own bedroom, upstairs. I am not perfectly steady yet because the leg is not quite back to normal, but it is coming, gradually. Little by very little! On June 16th, it will be three months since I walked normally. My osteoporosis is part of the cause for the sacroiliac problem. Now my days are filled with exercises of all sorts. We bought an exercise bicycle, which I ride at least 60 minutes every day (in two segments!). The therapist comes often to help me with the difficult exercises I can't do by myself. I get massages and keep trying to do some of the little things I used to do for myself . So I am trying seriously! We all are!

Two of our young African Sisters will be in the States this summer. One is from Kenya and one from Nigeria. We were invited by the SSND in North America to send two sisters to a Symposium being held in Milwaukee for SSND, and these two were chosen. Sister Ruth Emke, in our Development Office in St. Louis, decided to make the most of this opportunity, and planned some "events" in the nearby areas. She hopes to call attention to the growing SSND District of Africa and our needs. The two Sisters will be giving talks and even preparing some African food. Sister Nentaweh Wakger, from Nigeria, has a cell phone (#08035929199) if you want to call her to greet/welcome her. The second Sister from Kenya is Masicha Nasimiyu. By God's grace, Nentaweh should have flown out by now for Amsterdam and then Milwaukee.

Speaking of Development, I want to thank all of you who have been sending donations. I see your names on the list of Donors that comes in, and some are there very regularly. Thank you so much for your support! We are really very, very grateful. As we look to the future and the education of the young Sisters, we would be overwhelmed except for your faithful contributions. May God bless you abundantly!

This past year we have had two German volunteers here in Nigeria - part of a program organized by one of our sisters in Germany. One is in Gboko and one down here in Ikot Ekpene. They have been wonderful and have really enjoyed the experience totally! Although they were told they shouldn't come to Nigeria by some of their friends, all the bad things that they were told about the place have not been part of their experience. In the last month, each had some family members come to visit. Stephanie had her father and sister; Sarah had her mother and father. They, too, were so pleasantly surprised that Nigeria is not at all like the stories they hear. They were so pleased at the work the Sisters are doing. They encouraged us to write articles and send pictures out so that interested people could help. Both volunteers are returning to Germany in August to go to University. Sarah is talking of coming back. We will see! I certainly was a wonderful experience having them. And we appreciated the boost!

I am hoping to take my home leave in early September. We have a District Assembly at the end of August, and a weekend for the Temporary professed sisters in early September, so all hands are needed to help. I will be a secretary for the assembly. When I think of traveling, I do get nervous. I can't move fast, let alone run, and I don't have full control of my leg. I feel like I am on a stilt, without good balance. In fact, I cannot lift my left leg yet. Going up steps is slow – good leg first, and then pull the dull one. Going down is the reverse – dull leg first. So being in a crowded airport, rushing for a plane, carrying luggage – seem like a nightmare to me right now. I am praying that I continue to improve lots before then. Sitting more than 30 minutes is also stressful right now – the leg aches right down to my toes. So sitting for 5 hours on a plane has no appeal. However, I am taking one day at a time and entrusting the future to God.

There have been bulldozers clearing land very near to us for a housing development. We heard that there would be 250 plots available for anyone who wants to build. The government is apparently getting some roads in readiness first. Our quiet neighborhood will be changing! If the roads improve, we will be happy.

I am anxious to get this into the mail, so I will sign off here. My love and prayers to each of you!

Gabe

Celebration with ▶
the new African
SSNDs, 1999

◀ 1999 Area
leaders cutting
a celebration
cake at the SSND
African Fourth
District Assembly

2007-2019

Retirement

In retirement, Gabe remained active: leading Bible studies, helping with chores at the Villa, occasionally preaching, and serving wherever she was needed. She remained intellectually curious, politically informed, and intensely interested in others, especially her religious community and her family. Her increasingly serious health issues were not her major concern. Her SSND obituary stated what those who were fortunate enough to know Gabe already knew:

> *Sister Gabriel was a theologian, a teacher, a preacher, and a mother. She enriched many lives and was blessed with friends wherever she traveled. She was welcoming, wanted to hear everyone's thoughts and was a great believer in a person's goodness…. Sister Gabriel lived an extraordinary life, a life of wisdom and great generosity of spirit. She accepted death with faith and equanimity. She was thoughtful, prayerful and wise to the end. It was said that whole villages of Africa mourned her passing.*

How blessed we were to have known her.

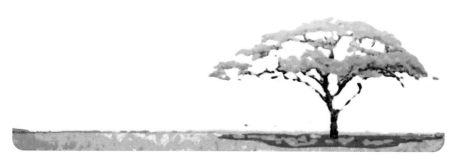

▲ At her 50th Jubilee celebration with Robbie Sabin, 2008

▲ Gabe with several members of her long-standing
Bible study group, including sisters Lois and
Carolyn at the far left, c. 2014

▲ October, 2016 Baltimore. Some of the SSNDs who served in Africa meet with the African Provincial Leader, Sr. Oyin-Oza Asishana. *Back row:* Sisters Virginia Brien, Anne Vogel, Oyin-Oza, Jane Irons *Front Row:* Sisters Gabriel, Dorothy Hunt, Betty Rosser

◀ Sr. Virginia Brien and Sr. Gabriel with Sr. Vicky Swanzy-Essieu of Ghana in Baltimore, 2017

▲ The Province of Africa celebrates the installation of the third Provincial Council, August 28, 2019

▲ Assembly of students in front of the new building, to be named for Sister Gabriel at the Notre Dame Secondary School Mkar, 2018

Her Legacy

Sister Gabriel's life and work in Africa lives on in three areas where she served.

The Church of Nigeria

Nigeria is home to some 29 million Catholics, the second largest population of Catholics in Africa. It boasts one of the highest number of priests in Africa. The two seminaries where Gabe ministered, St. Joseph (Minor) Seminary, Zaria, and St. Augustine's Major Seminary, Jos, are still in operation.

Of the young men and women taught by Gabe in Nigeria's seminaries and the SSND formation programs, many still serve the Church there. The theology as well as the Christian life lessons she taught live on. In a happy twist, many parishes in the U. S., including parishes in the Archdiocese of Baltimore, welcome young Nigerian priests to minister in their parishes. These men, products of the Nigerian seminary system, may have been indirectly touched by Gabe, who may have taught their teachers.

Notre Dame Secondary School Mkar

Today Notre Dame Secondary School (NDSS), Mkar is thriving and, in fact, celebrating the 25th anniversary of its founding. It is known nationally for the quality of its education. Bishop William A. Avenya, Catholic Diocese of Gboko, reflected this high regard in his letter of condolence on hearing of Gabe's death:

> *We received with grief, but appreciation to God, the news of the passing on to glory of your beloved Sr. Gabriel Roeder,*

SSND. We recall that she was one of those instrumental in the establishment of Notre Dame Secondary School, Mkar...iconic in our locality, not only in the provision of quality education, but also in the empowerment of the girl child. The Catholic family of Gboko deeply commiserates with you over this painful loss.

Currently, a new classroom wing at NDSS is under construction. The principal Sr. Theodorah M. Ihiro, SSND, writes:

We are building a structure of new classrooms which is named after Sr. Gabriel. We started its foundation at the time when Sr. Gabriel died. This was very significant to us at Notre Dame Secondary School Mkar because it reflects what Sr. Gabe dearly dedicated her life to when she was here: directing construction of quality structures on our school premises with a view to ensure quality education of a girl child.

The SSND African Province

In 2011, the Province of Africa of the School Sisters of Notre Dame was established. Today, it includes 85 women living in 23 communities and serving in six countries. Among the women Gabe taught is the current Provincial Leader, Sr. Oyin-oza Asishana, SSND, who writes movingly of Gabe's involvement in her formation:

Sister Gabriel was a great helper who was very attentive to the needs of others always for the good of everyone; this I discovered in 2001 when she was teaching us Christology, Mariology and scripture in the Postulancy in Mbribit.... As postulants she led us into life even in tough ways and lived a life of simplicity always attentive to our needs. She was a gracious asset to community life, who trusted God in every circumstance of her life and always encouraging us to presume the goodwill of the other. This was visible in *how she took life one day at a time. Sister was very easy to live with and easy to interact with. She respected and appreciated the uniqueness in each person.*

Sister Gabriel gave her all in creating the Province of Africa from her time in formation to serving in the then District of Africa. I can rightly say that she was one of the strong beacons that form a firm foundation for the Province. She quietly preached the Good News and made lots of sacrifices in order to touch lives in Africa especially in Nigeria. She gave her ALL....

During the times I visited Gabriel in Baltimore, even in her frail state, I always felt a sense of community in her and in the reality of our lives in mission. I felt like she was with me back home in Nigeria. She was never tired of giving.... Her gracious spirit, her efficacious smile, her gift of presuming the goodwill of the other, her wisdom, and her sense of compassion and solidarity will forever be remembered. Even in death, she was still giving...and she gave up everything!

How blessed are we, like the sisters she taught, to have known and been enriched by Sr. Gabriel Roeder.

▲ Sisters rejoice at the establishment of the School Sisters
of Notre Dame Province of Africa on August 28, 2011

Mure U Tiv

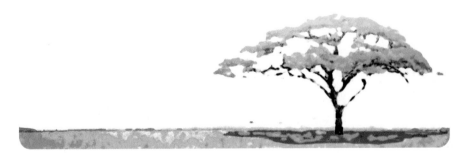